paola
de pietri

paola de pietri

istanbul
new stories

steidl

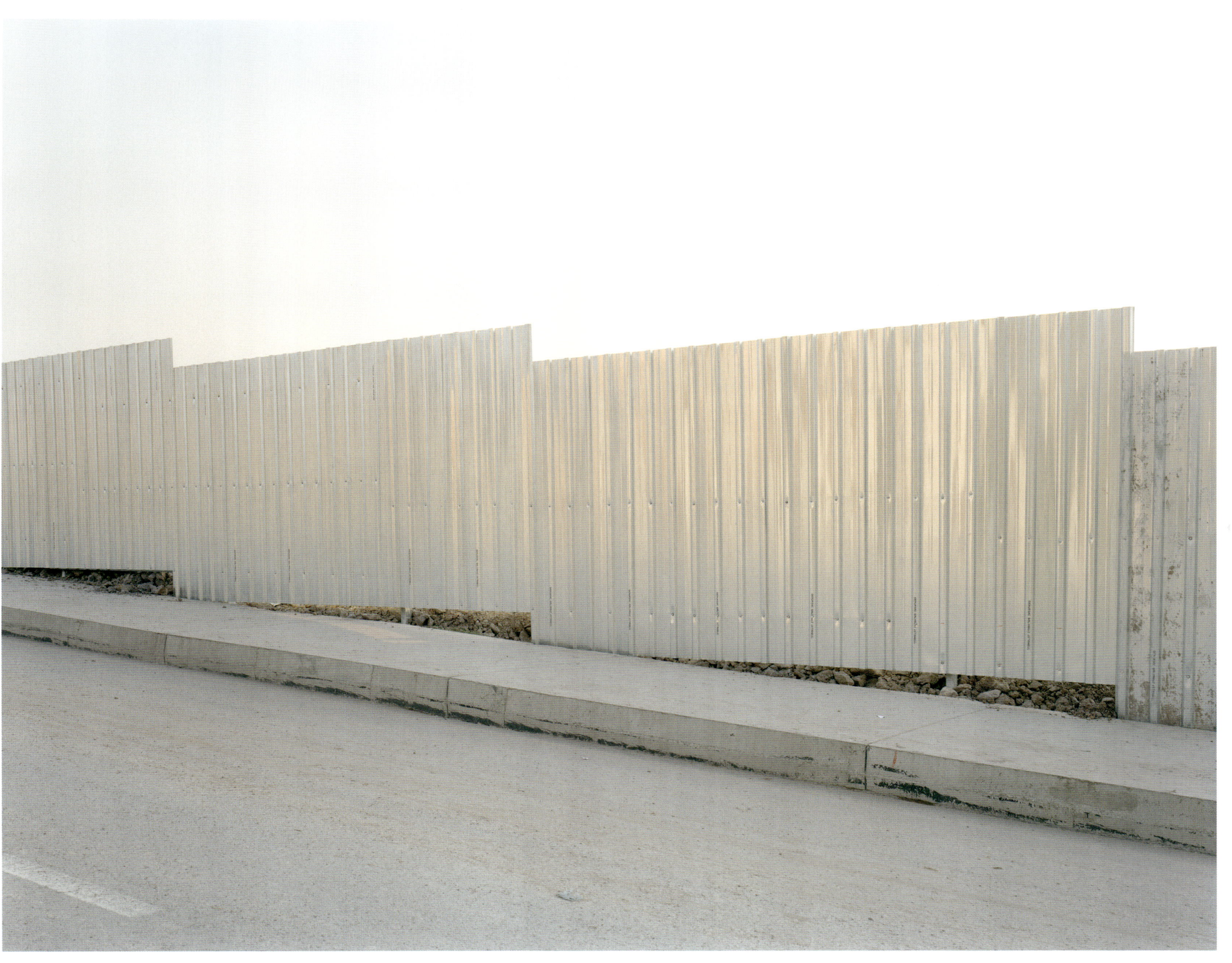

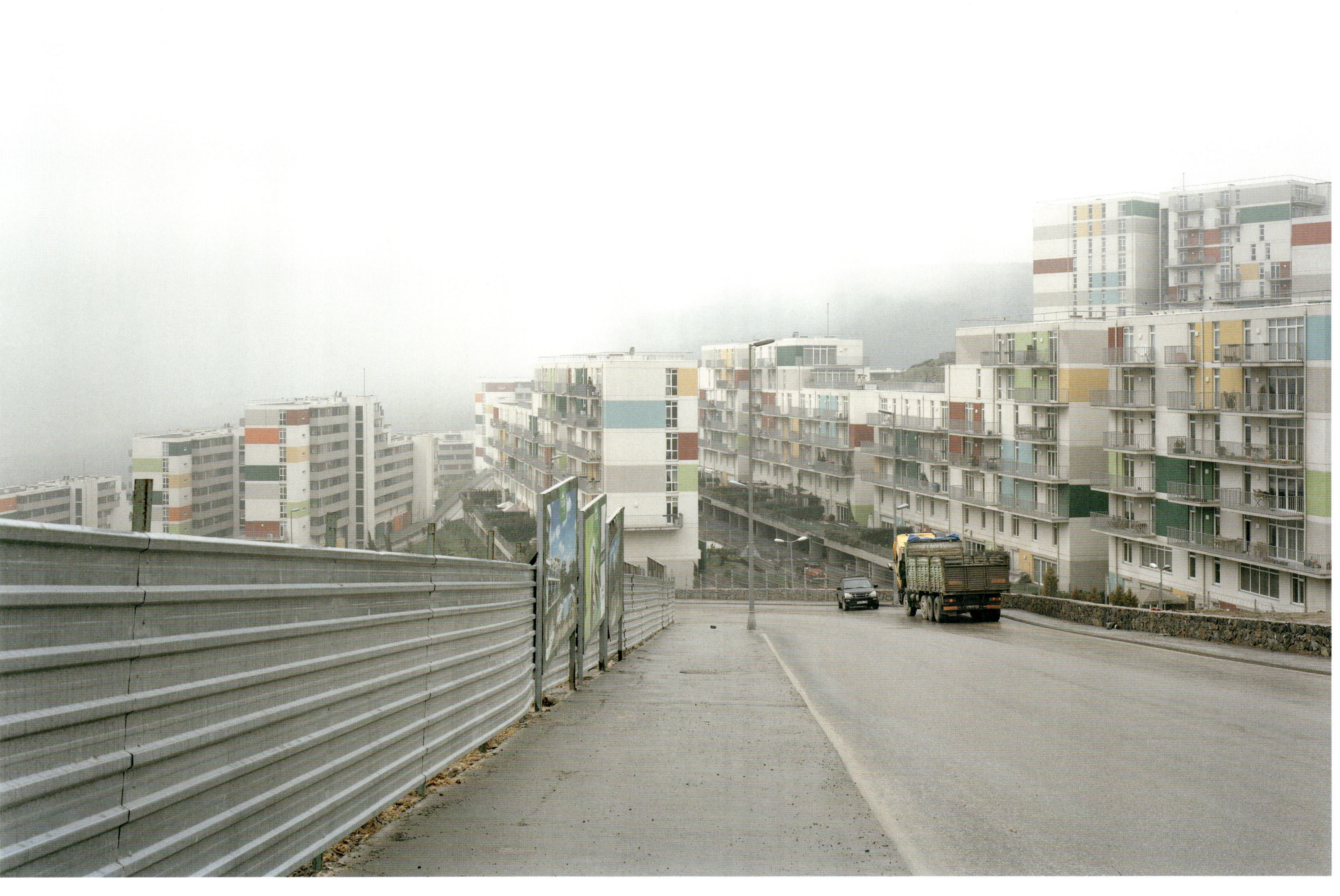

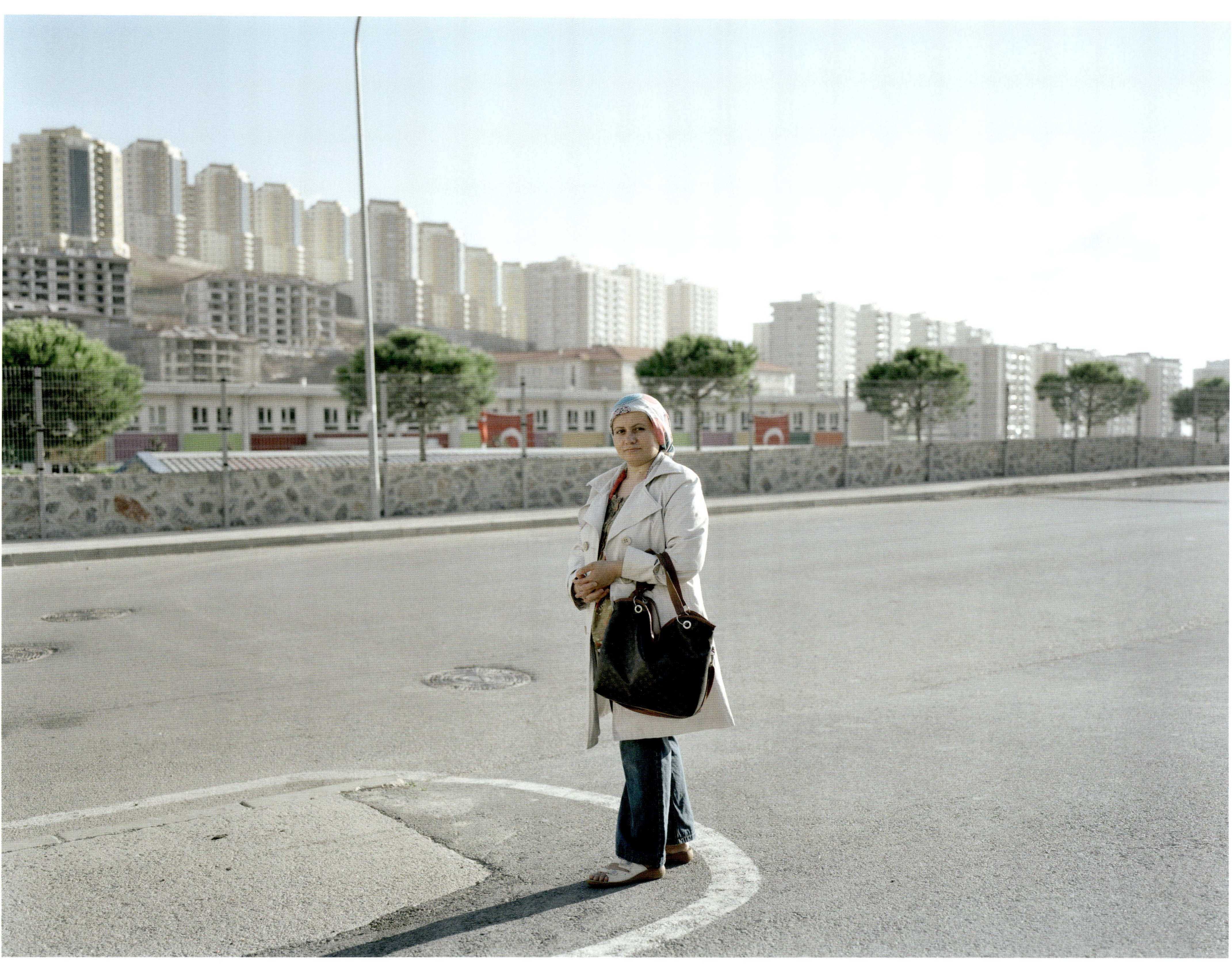

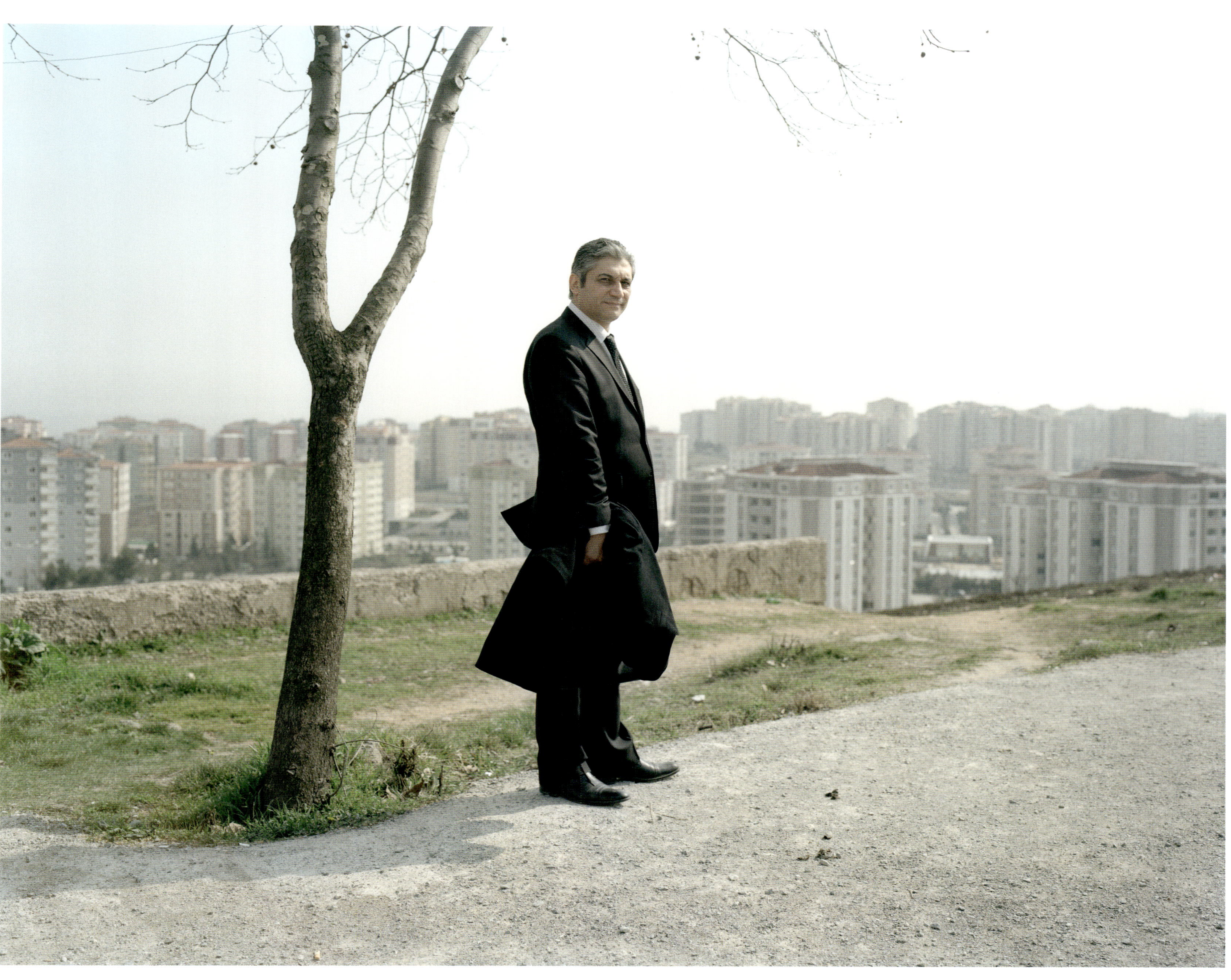

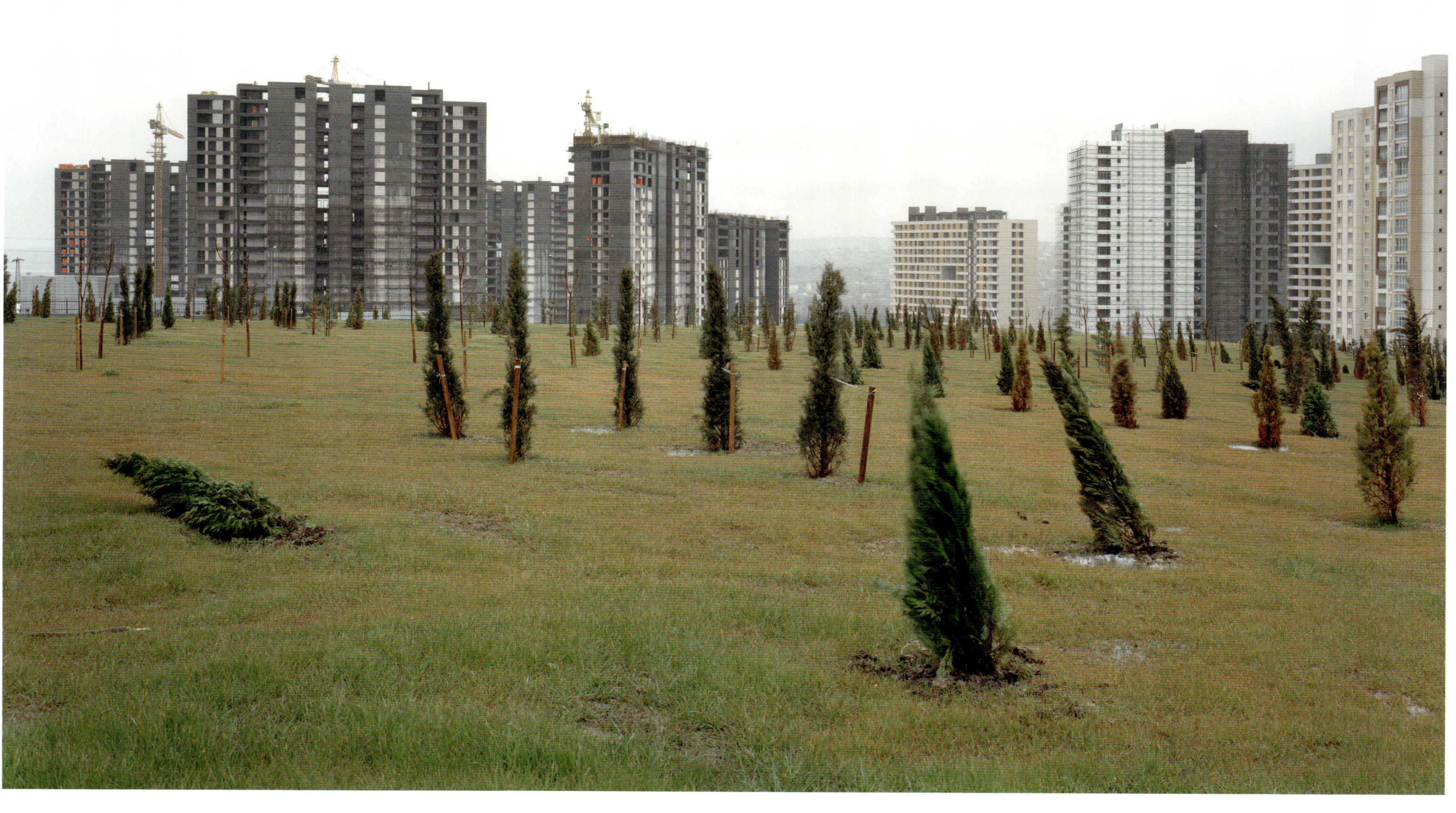

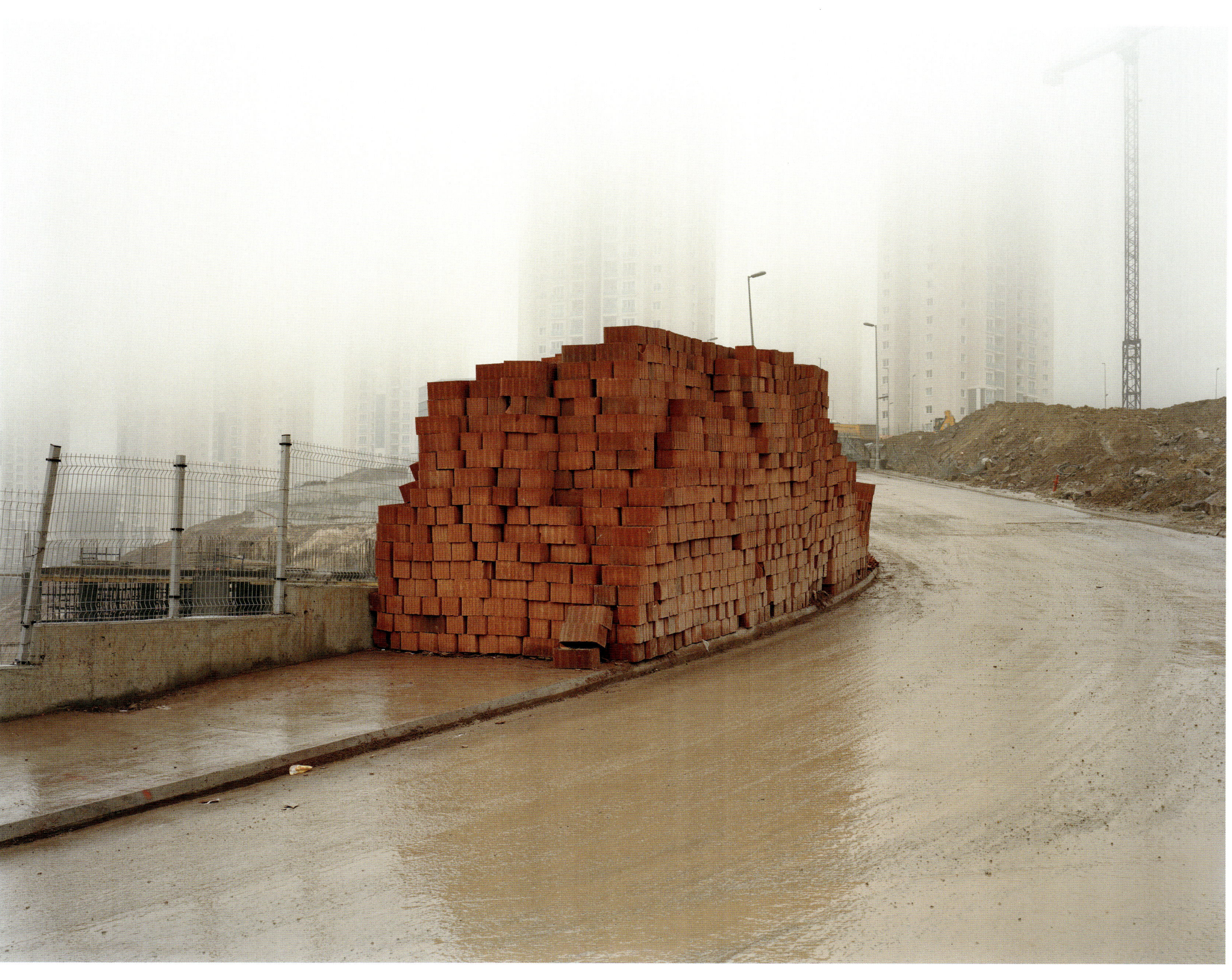

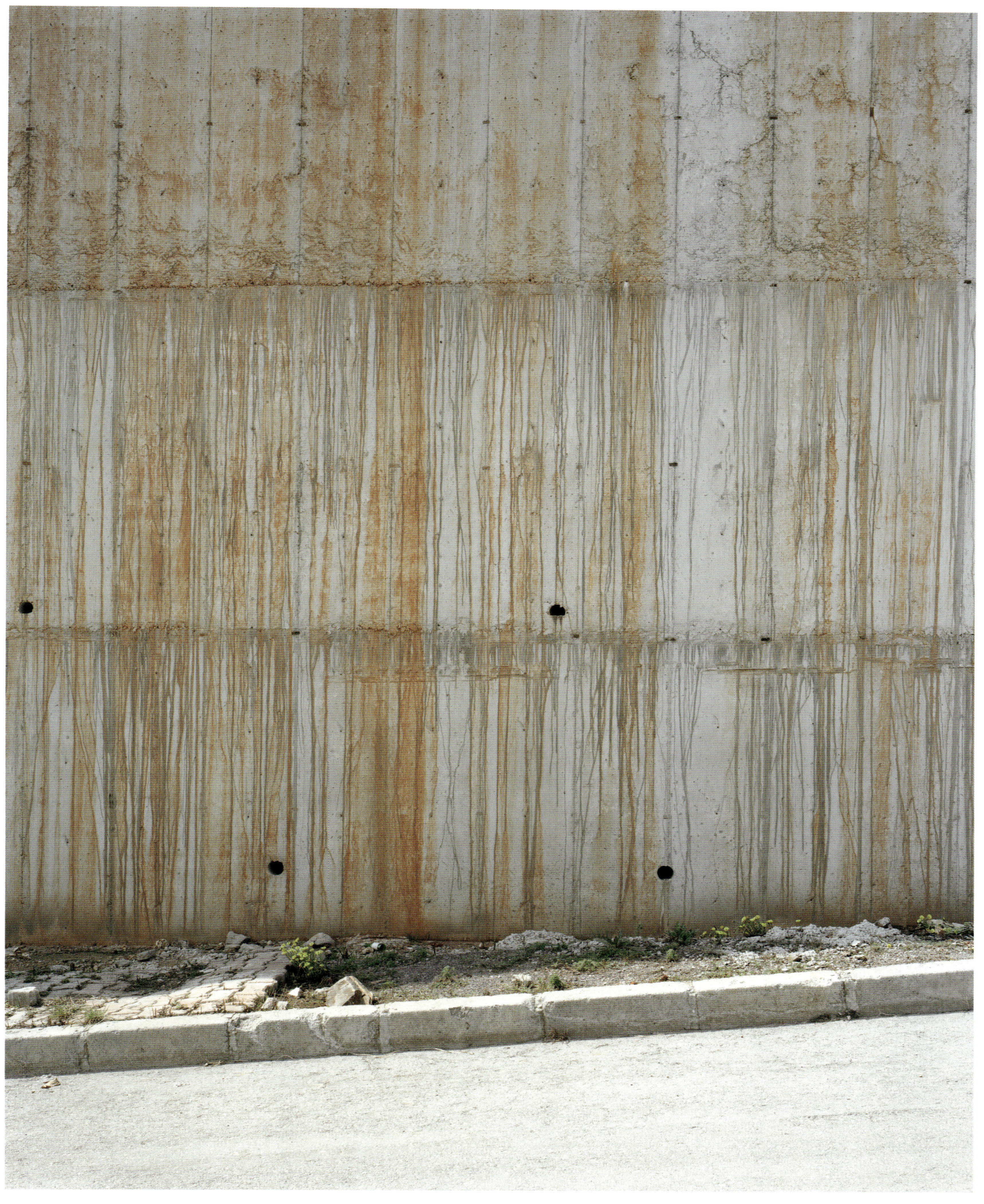

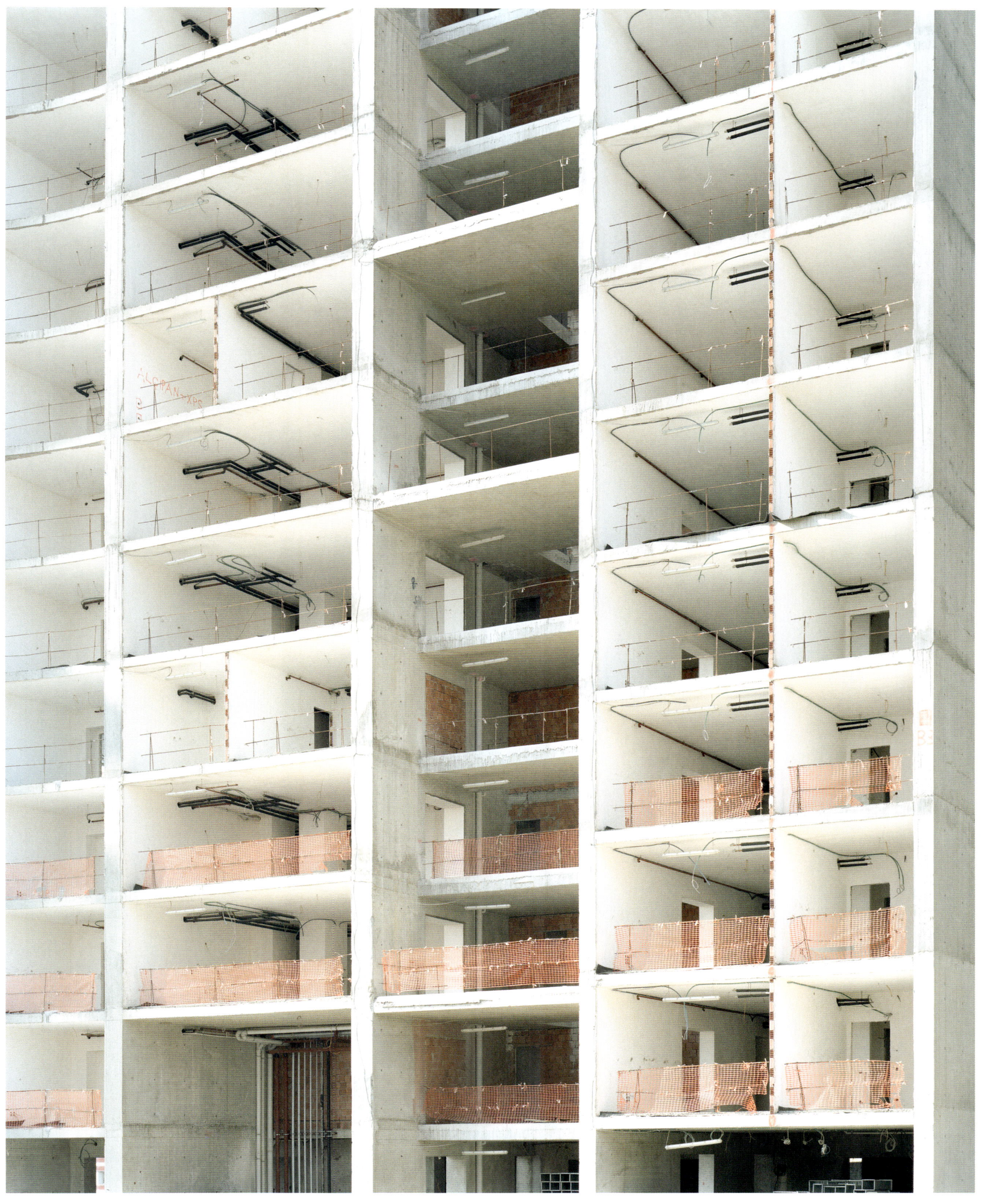

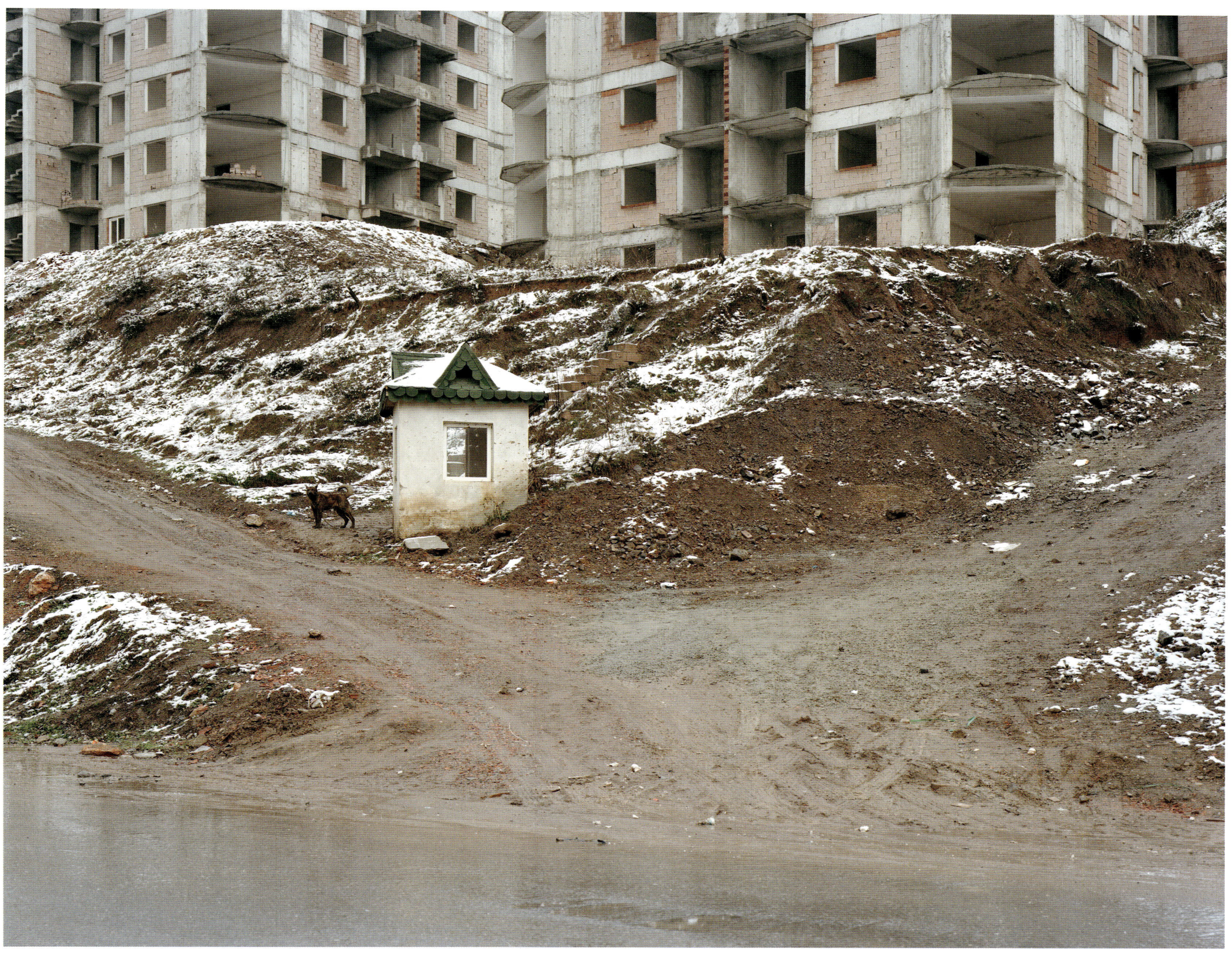

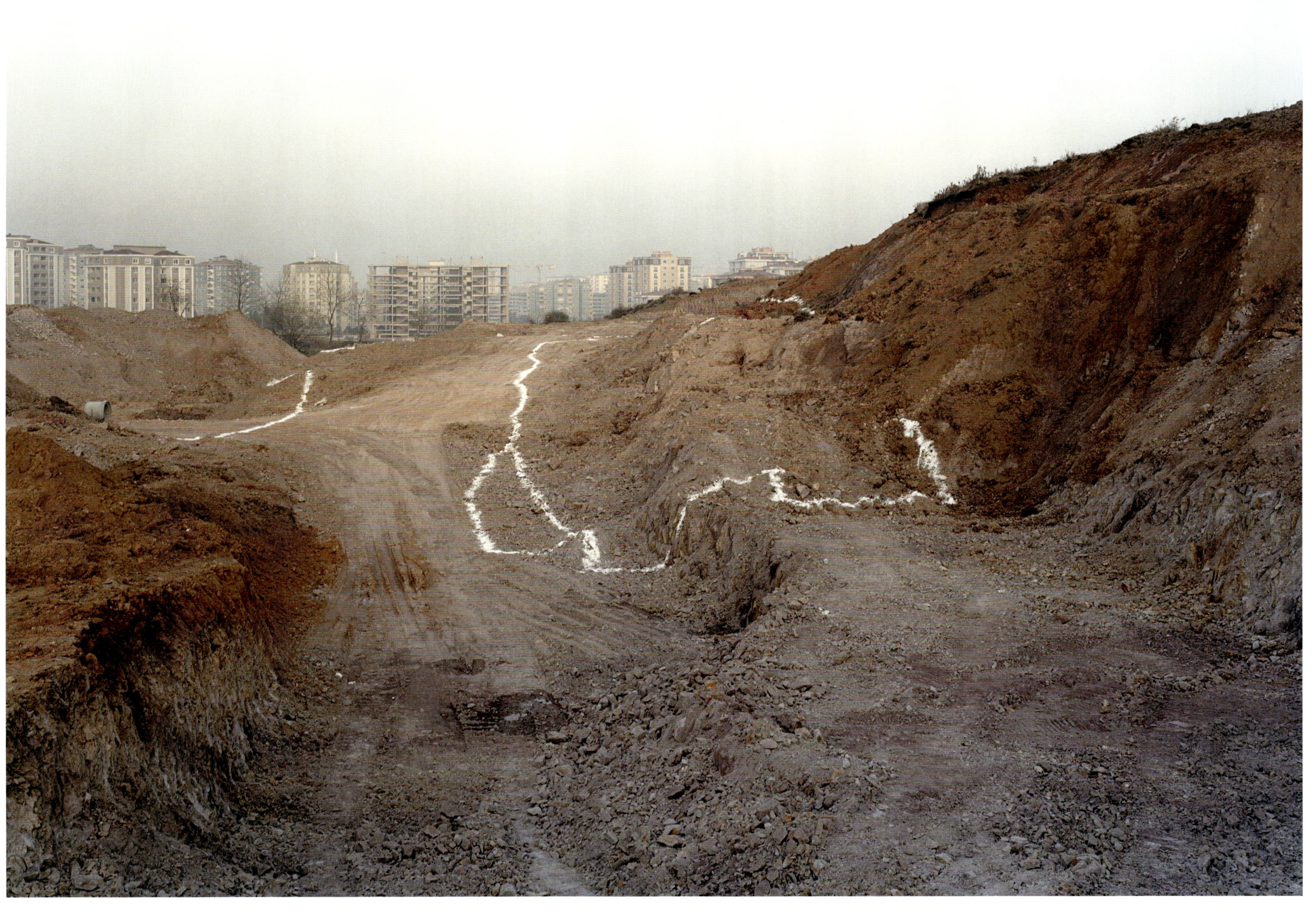

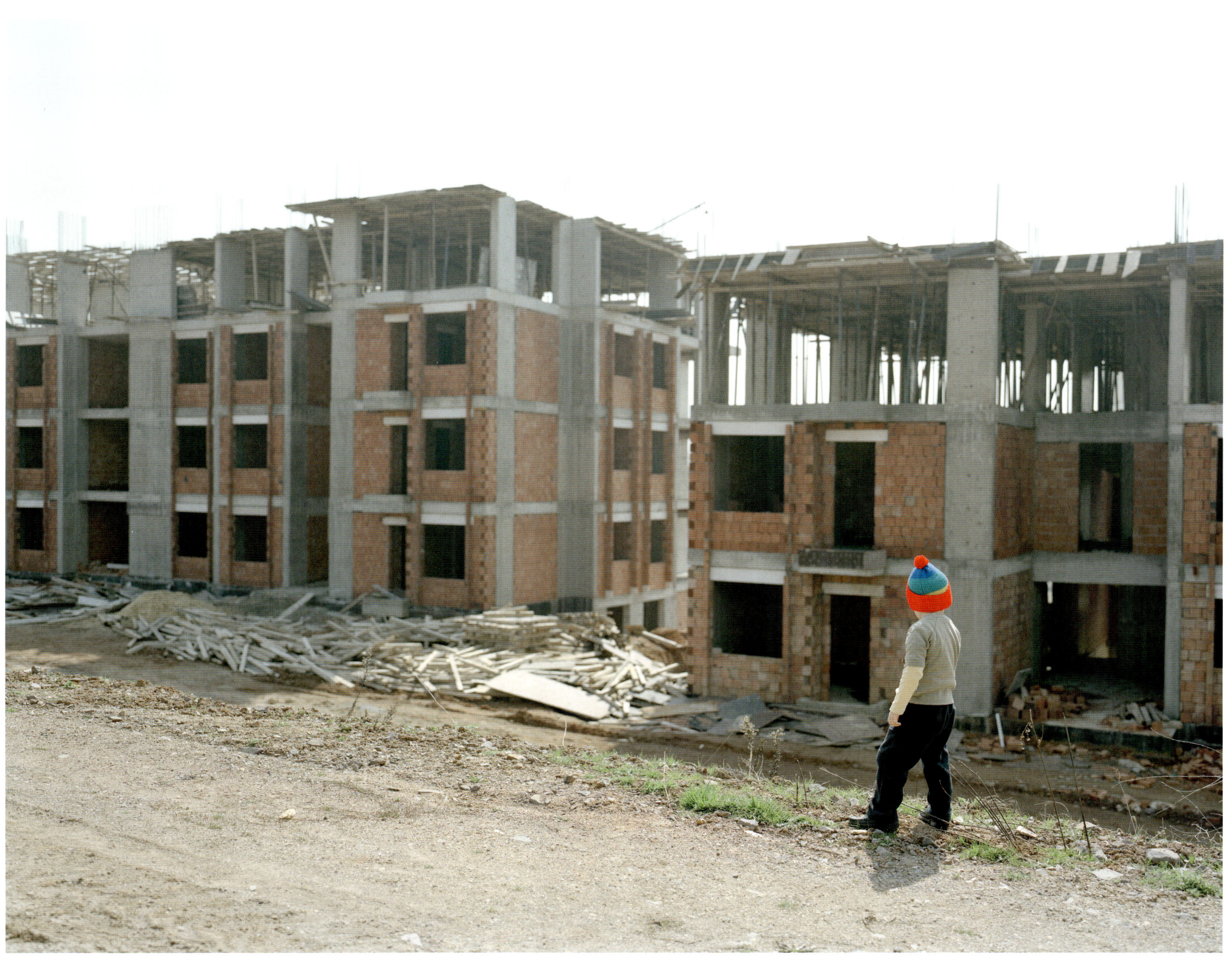

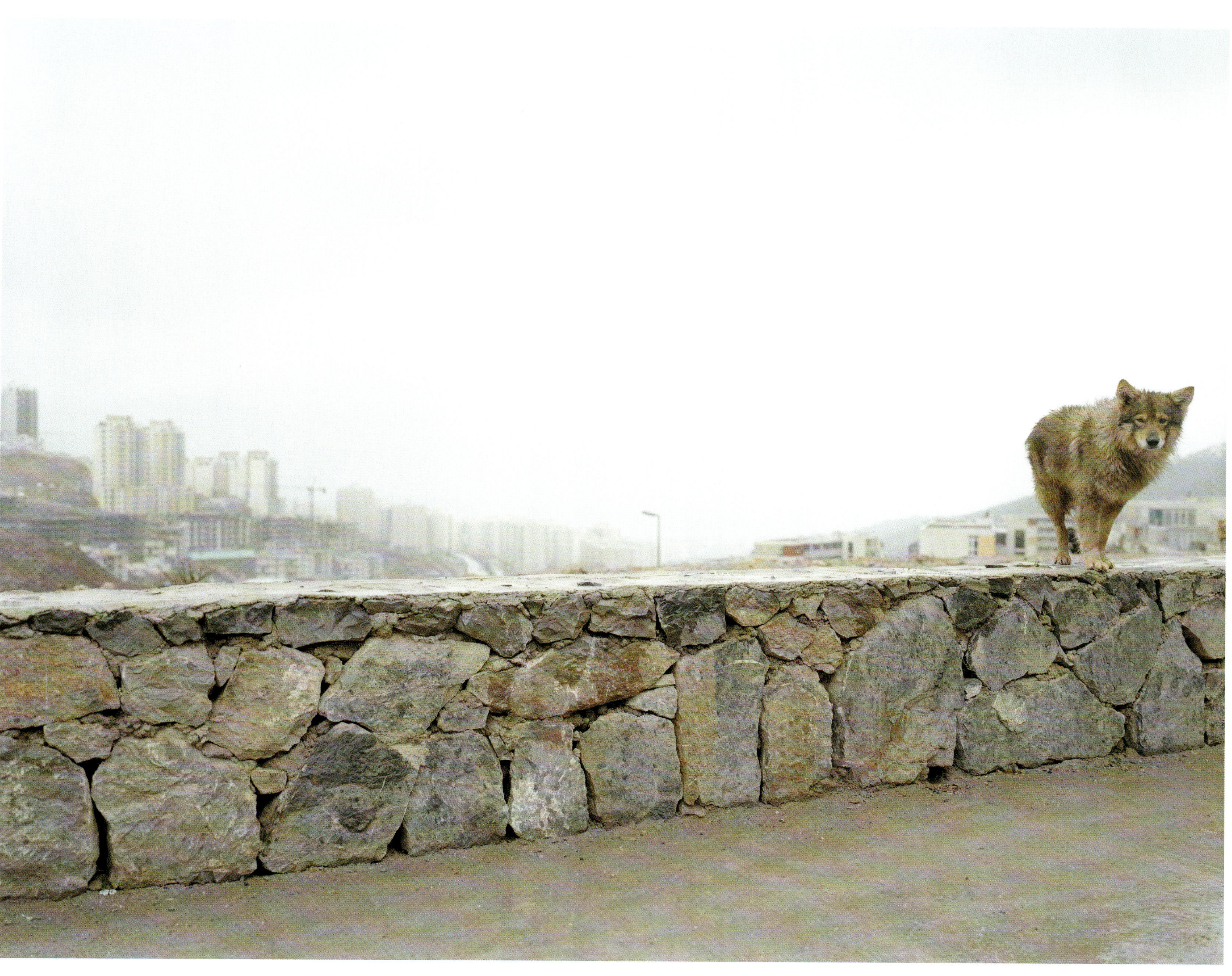

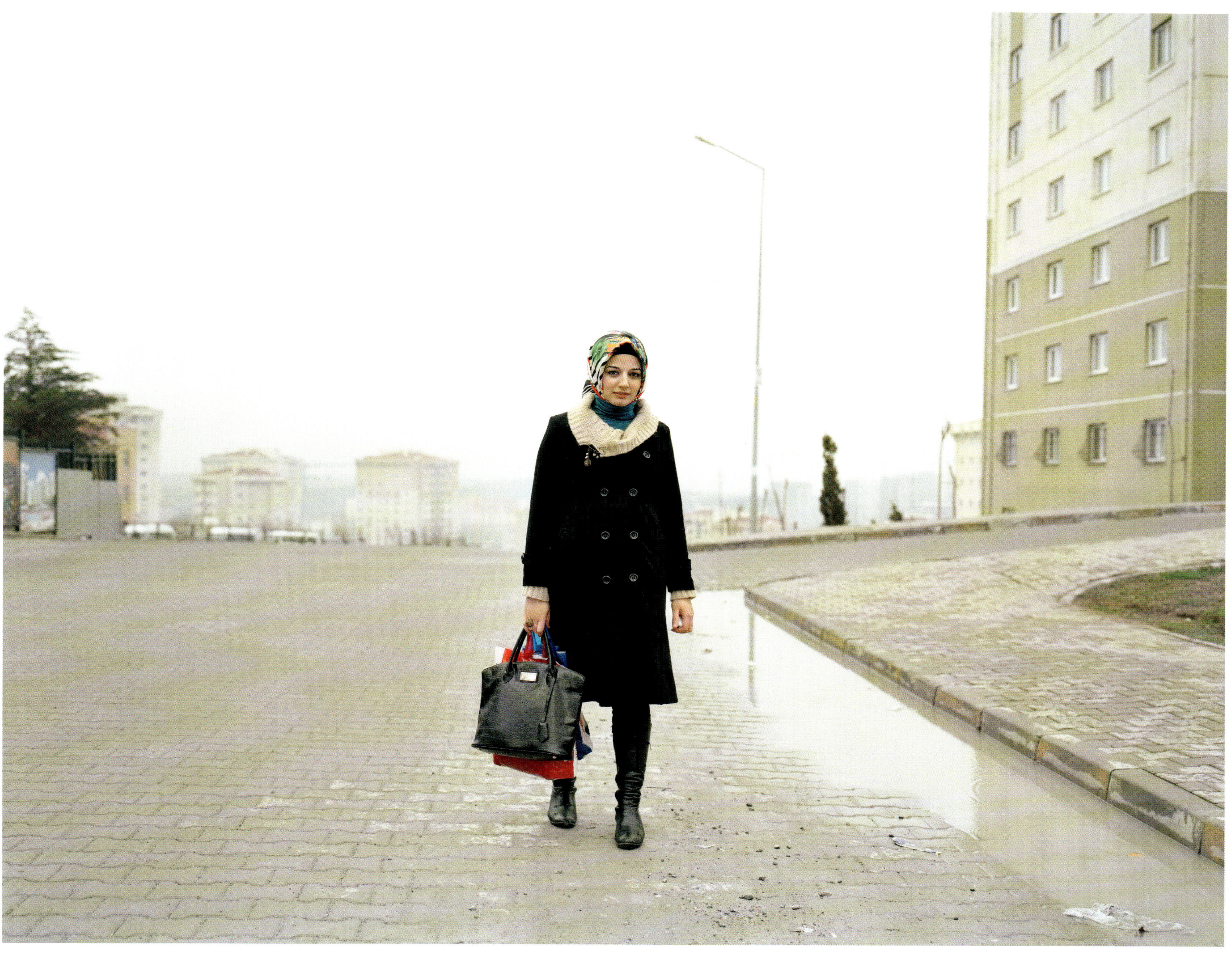

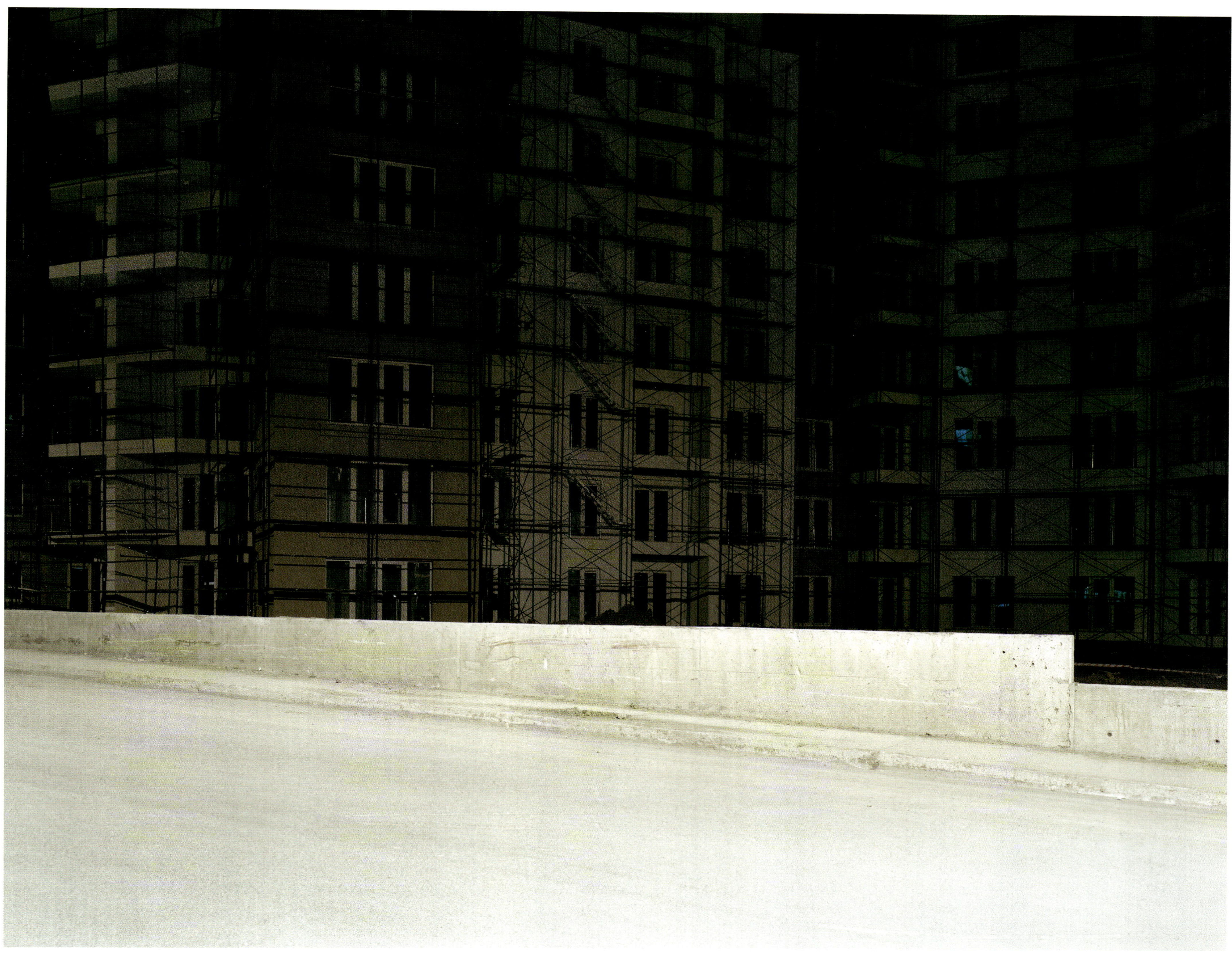

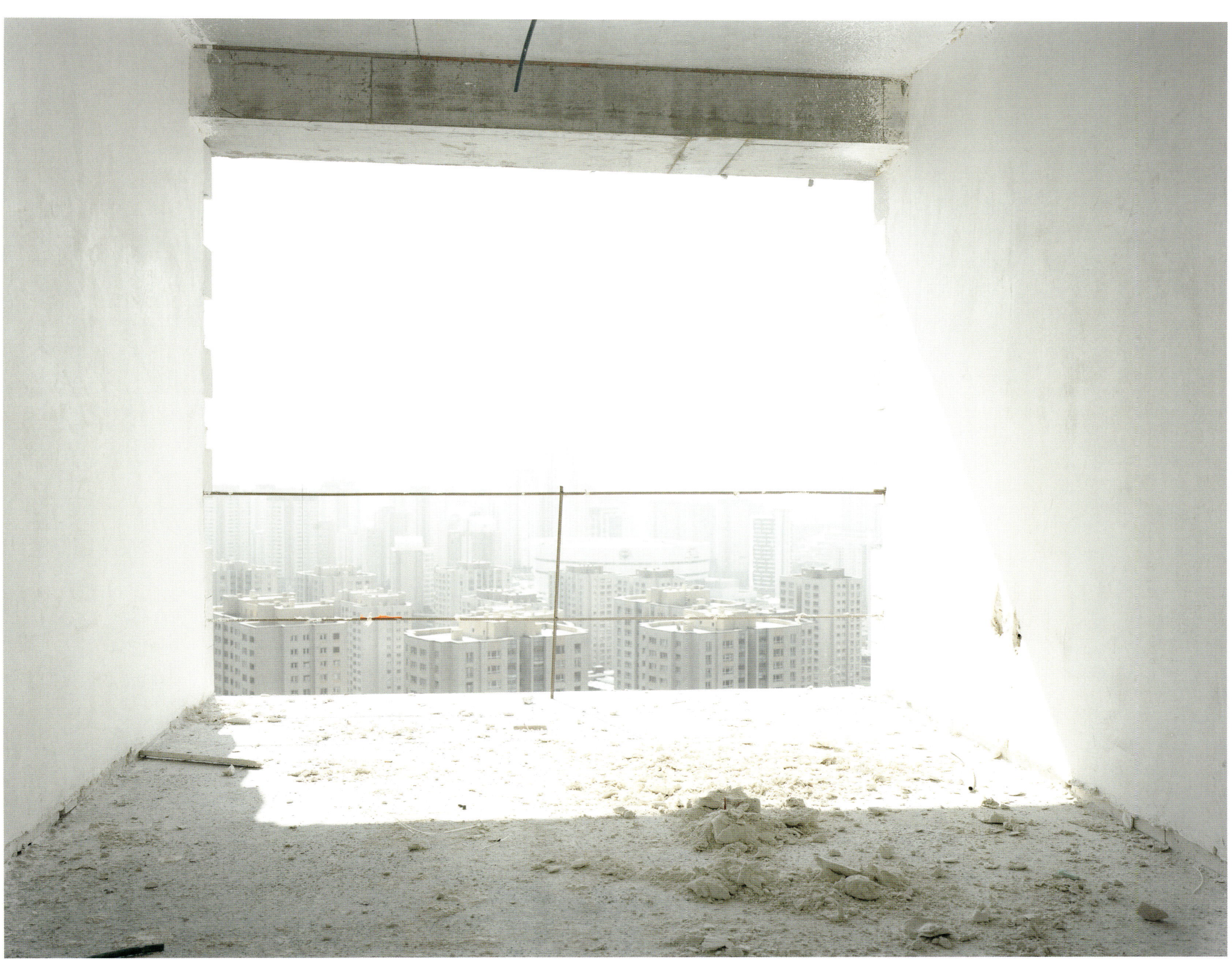

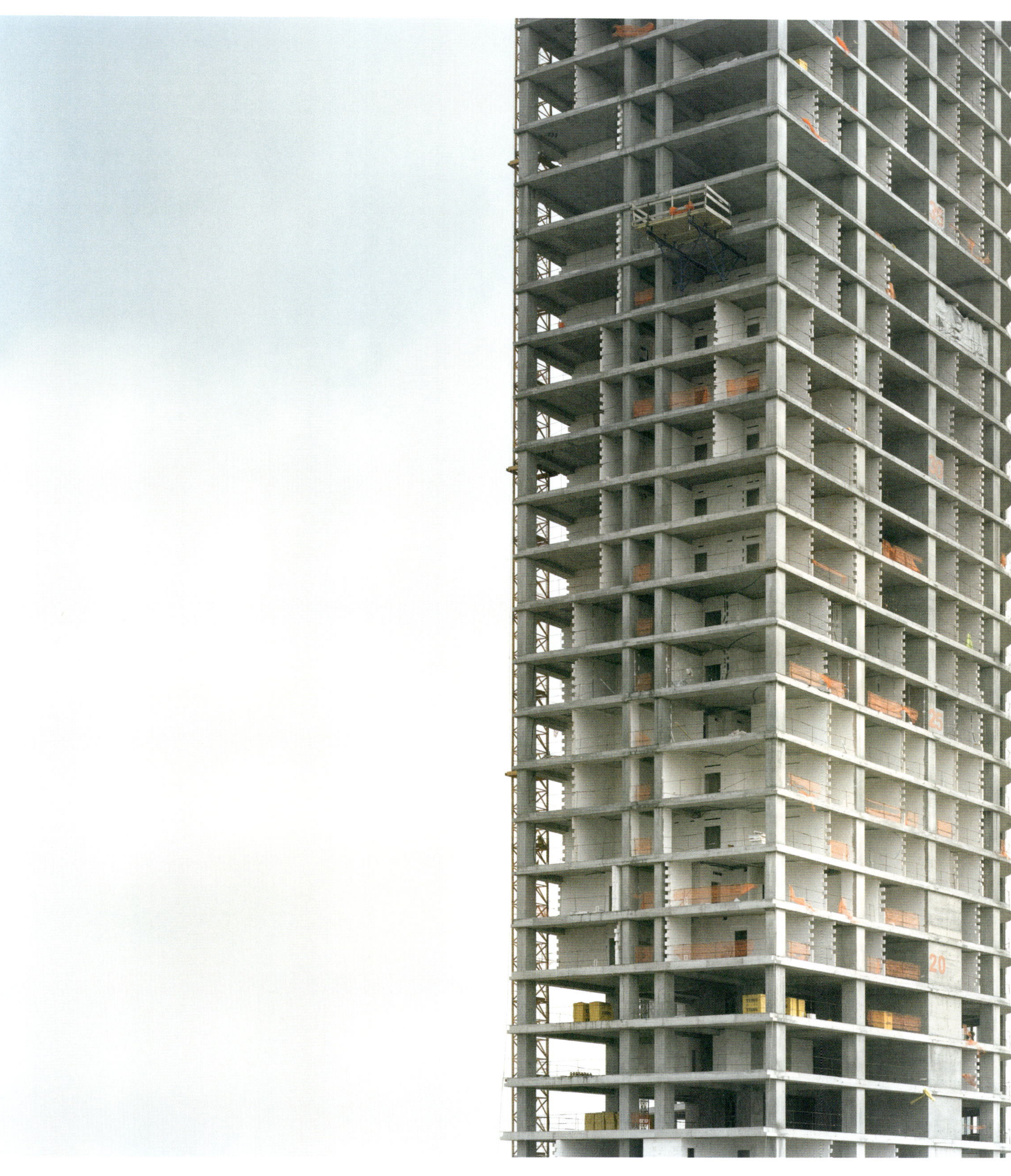

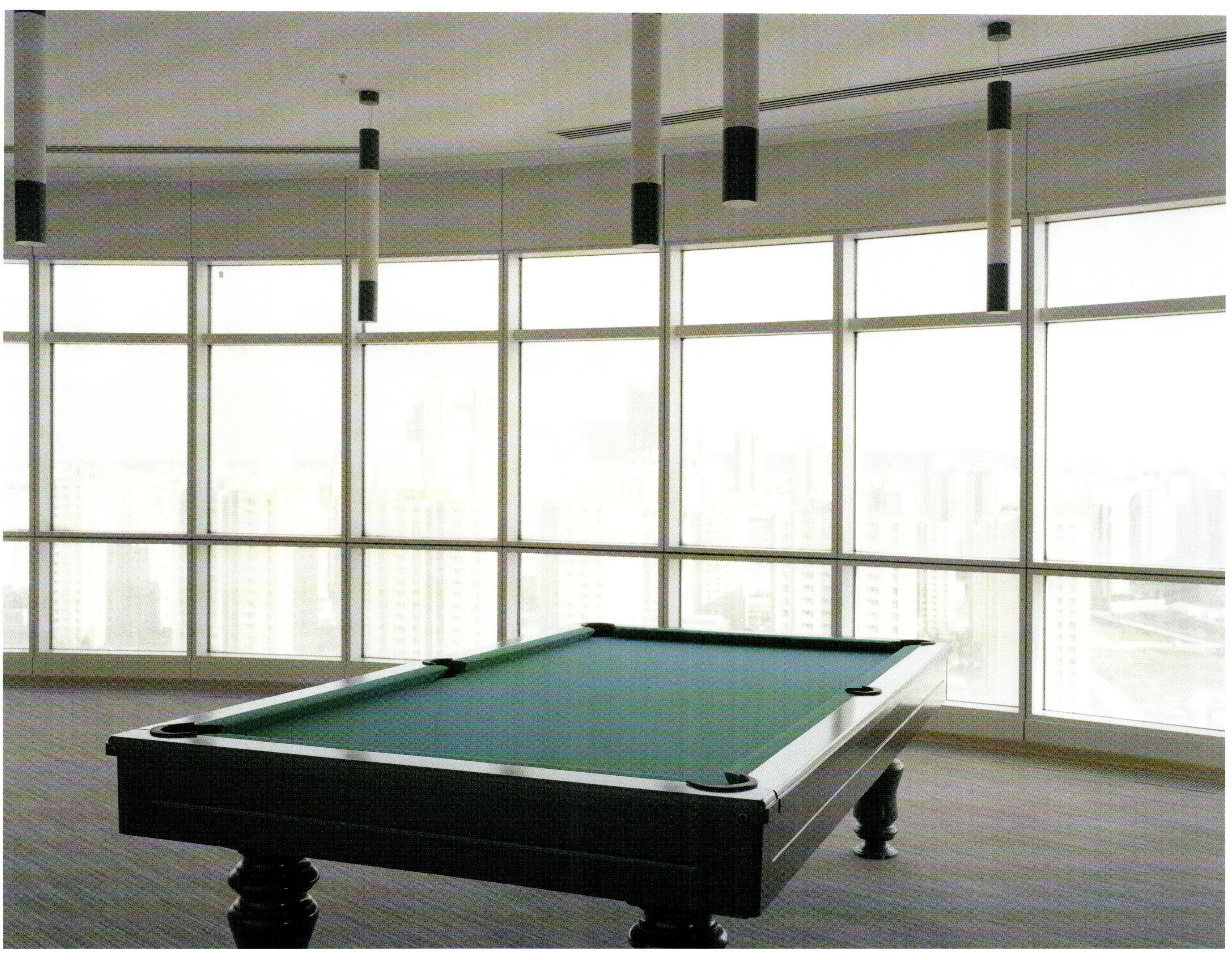

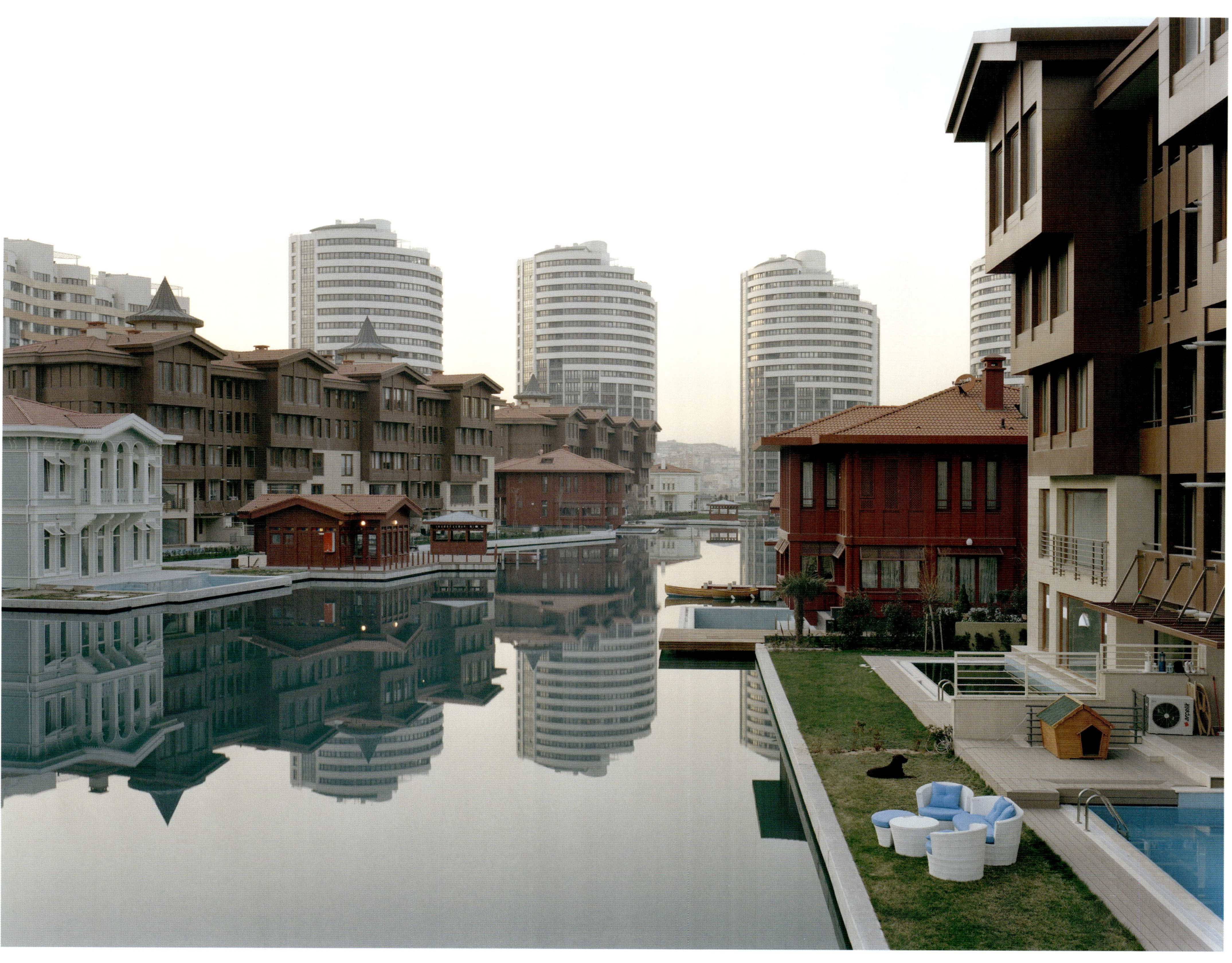

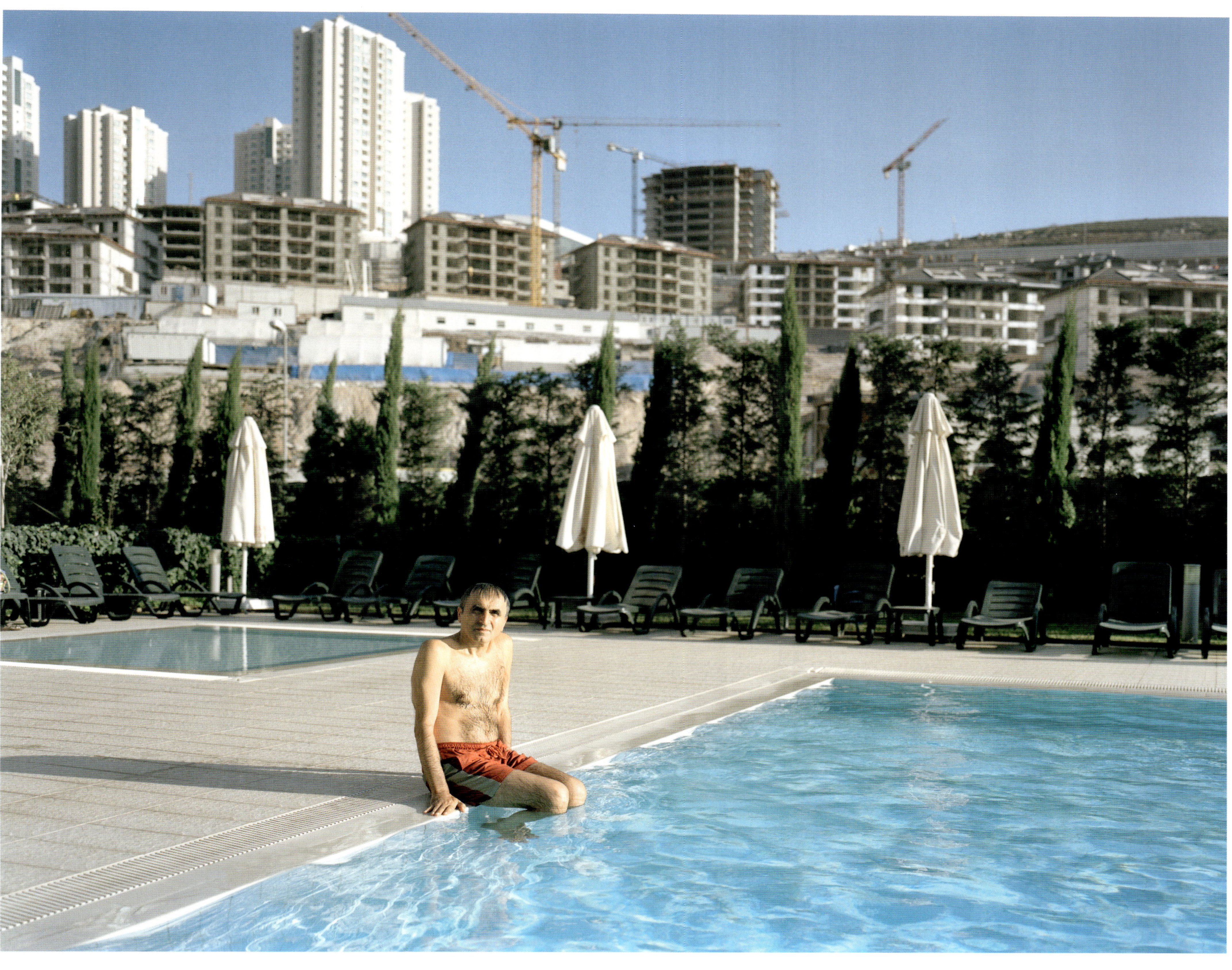

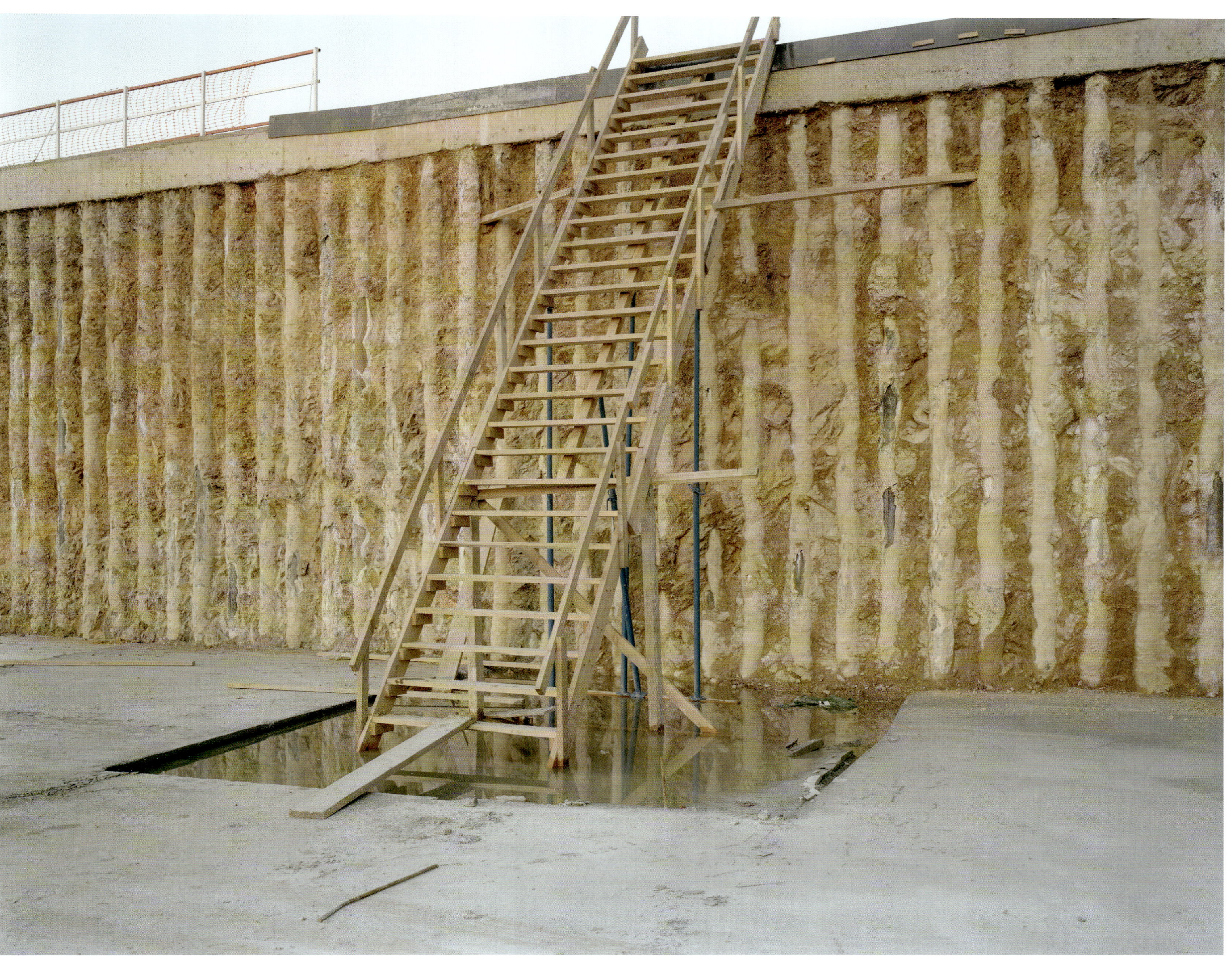

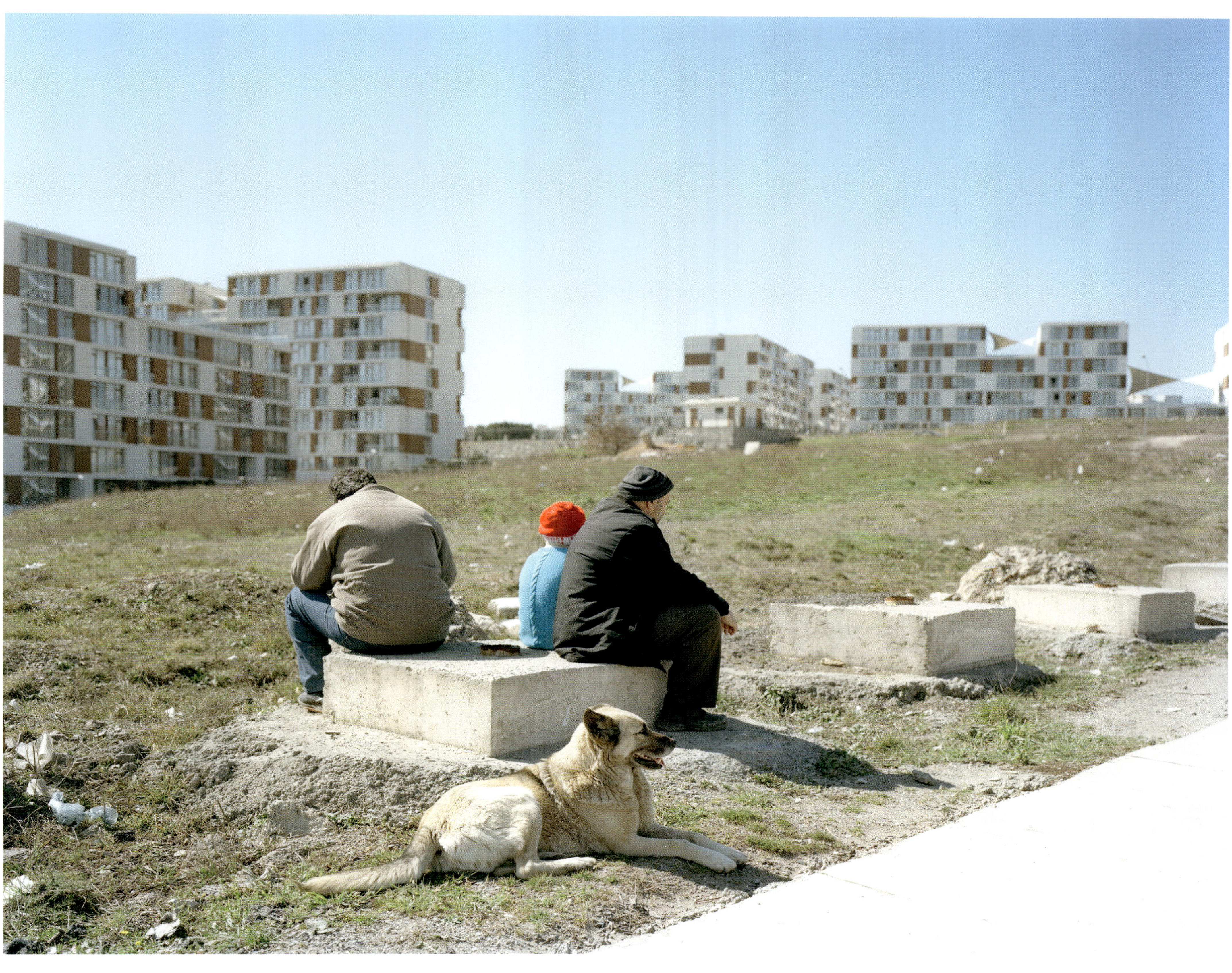

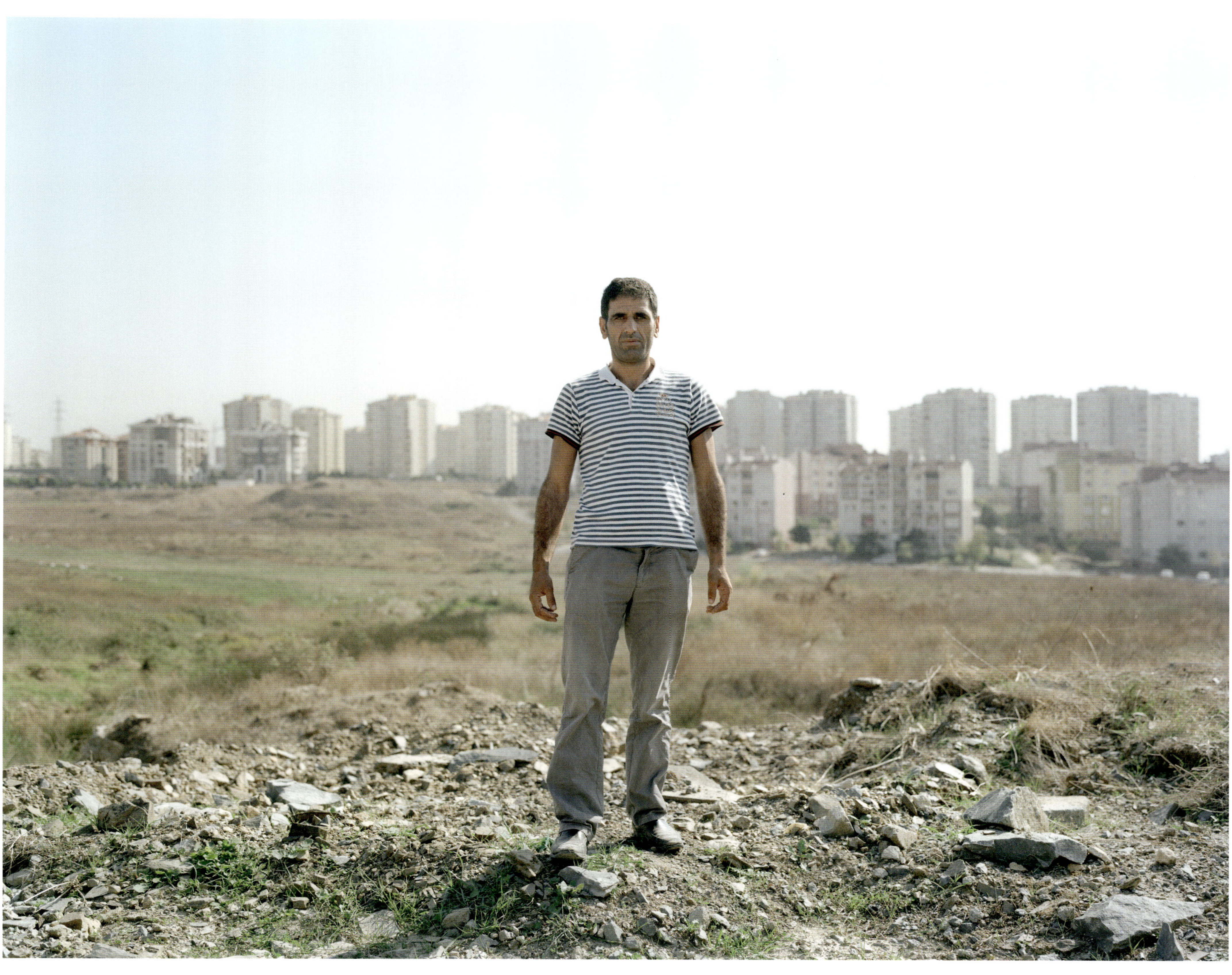

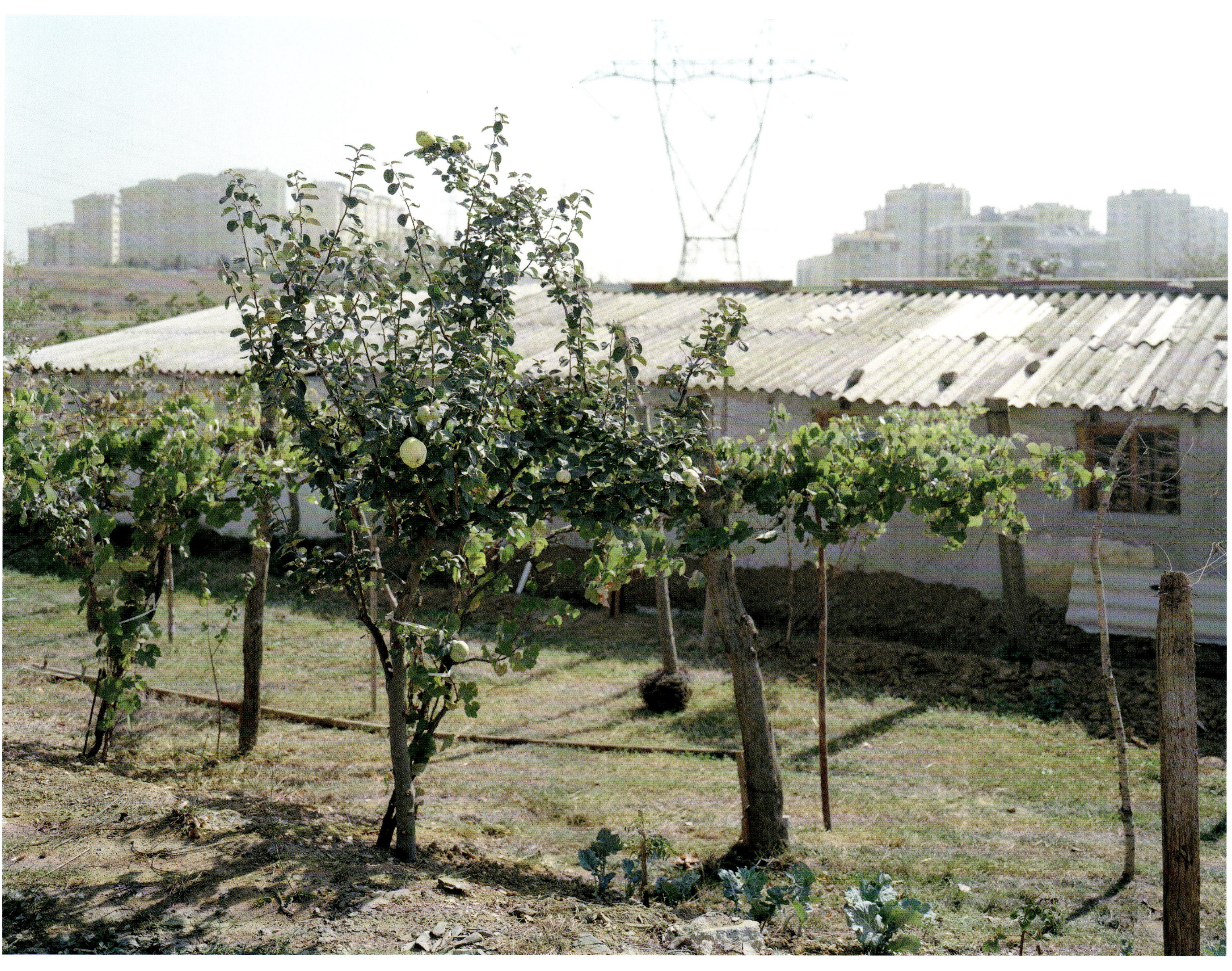

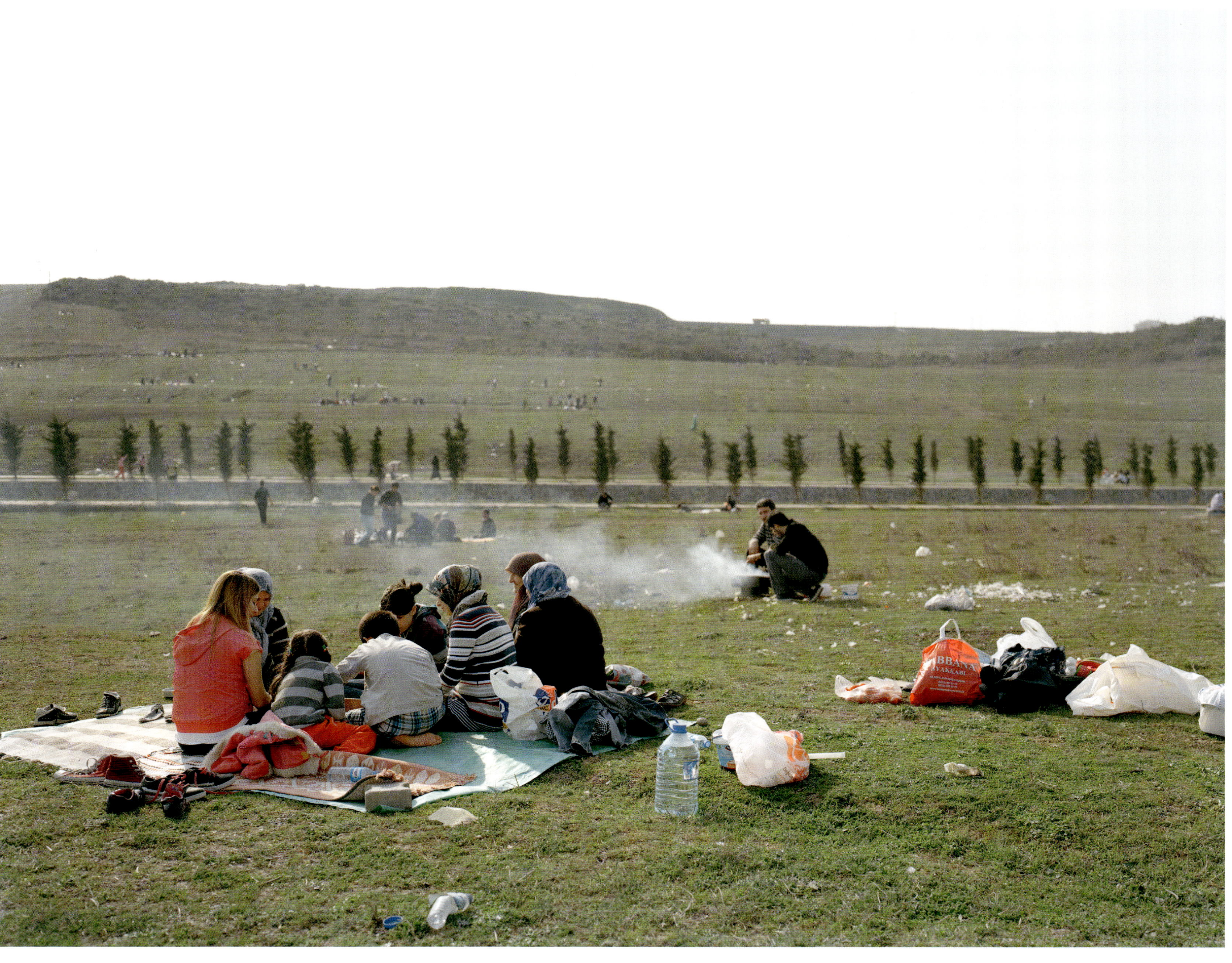

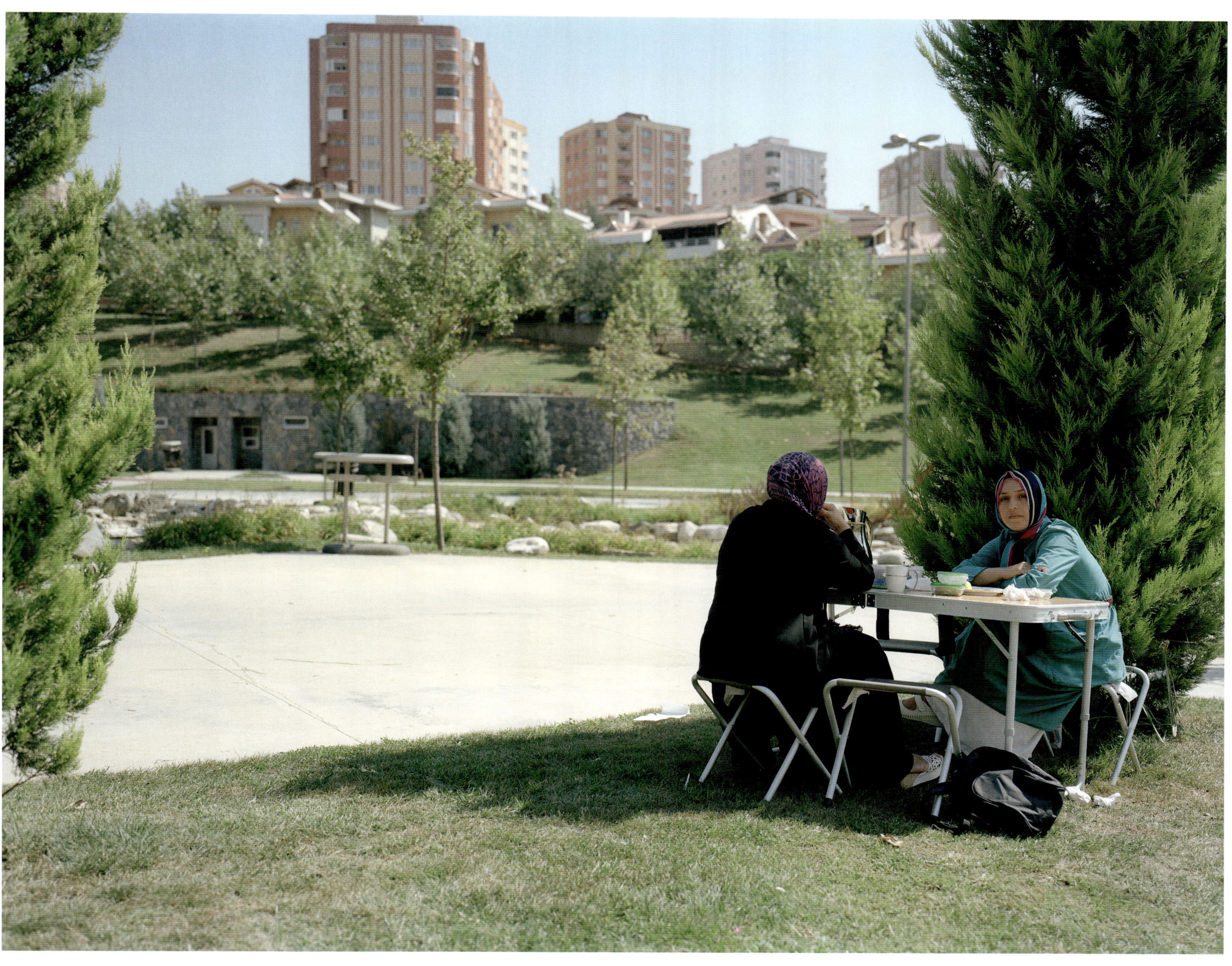

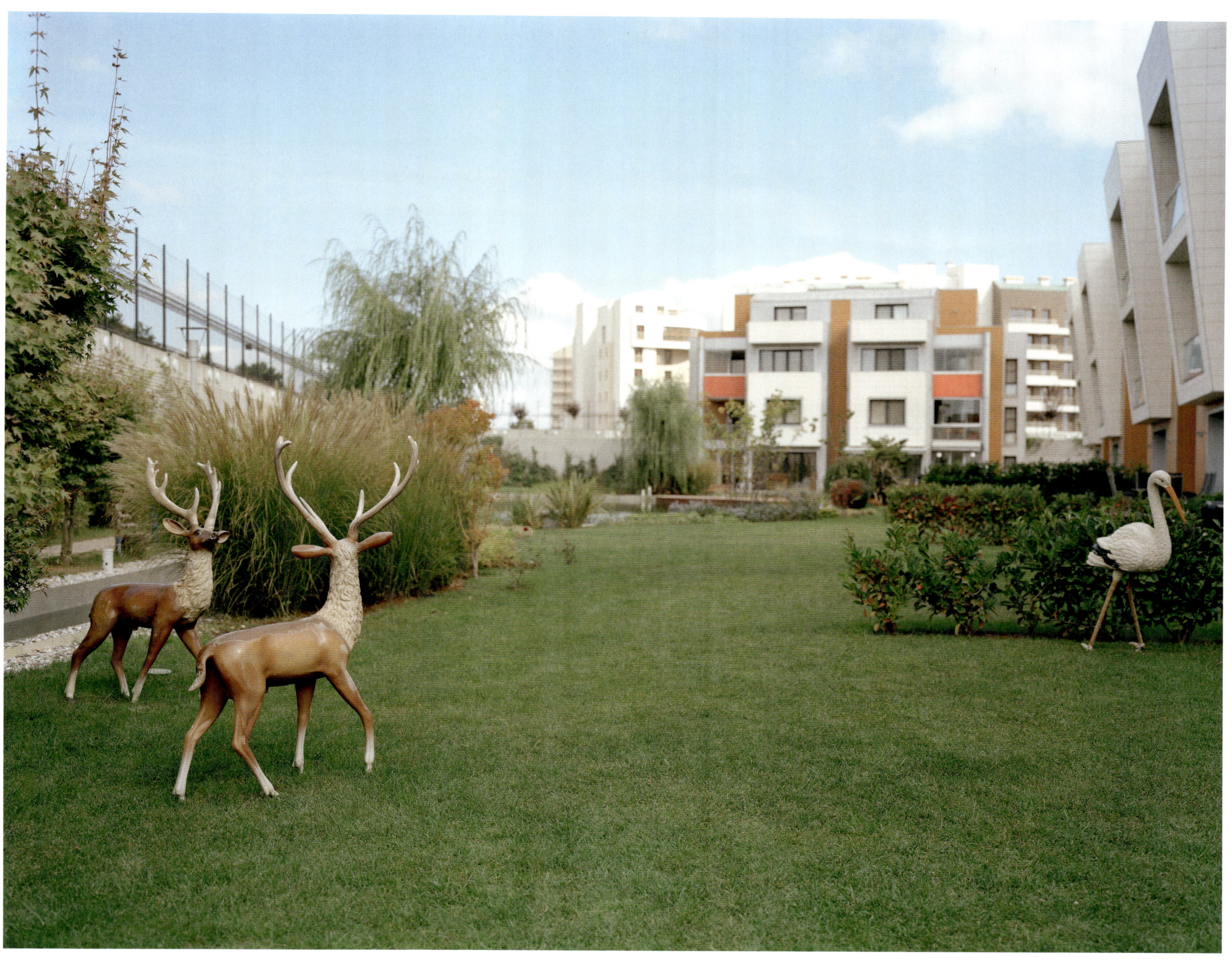

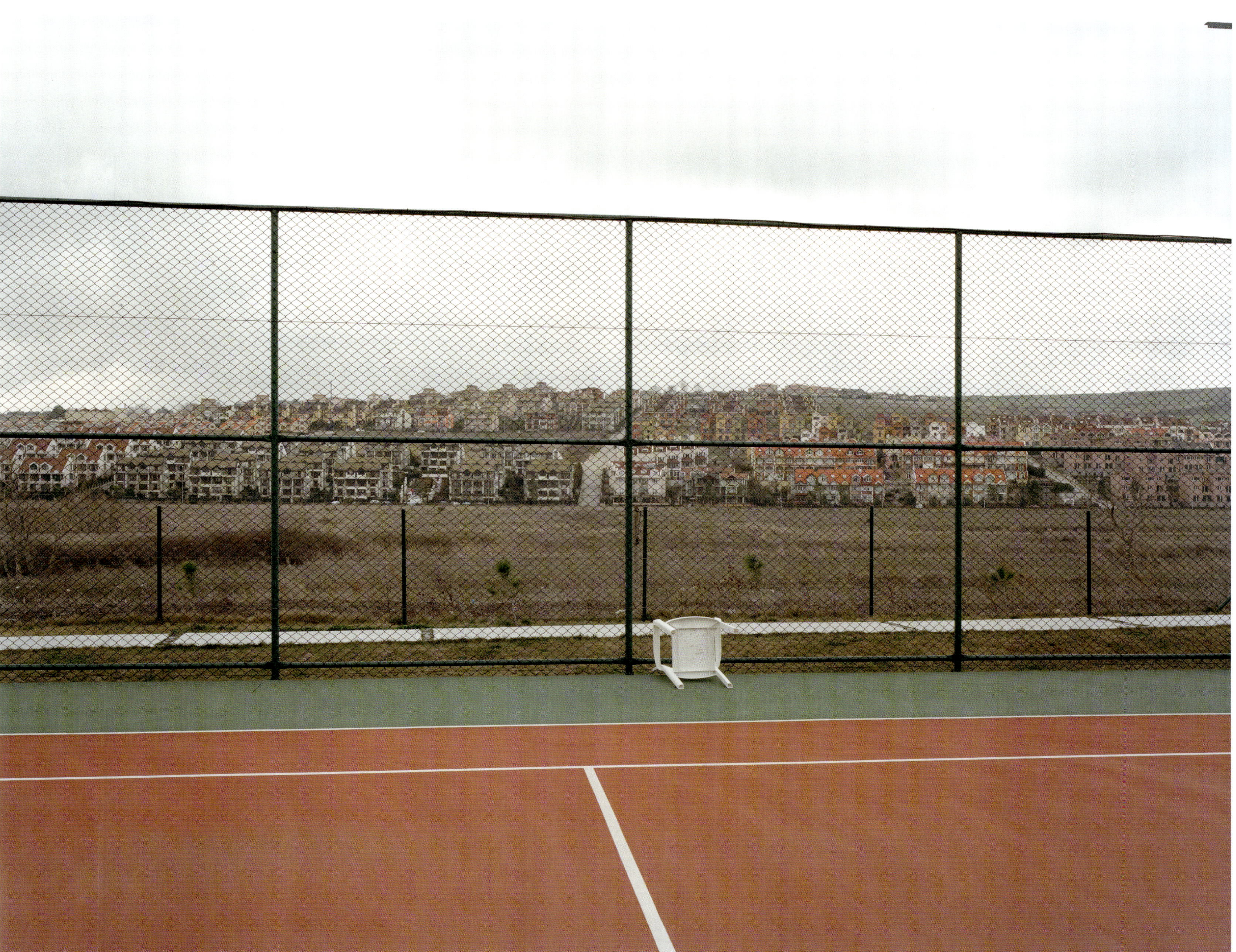

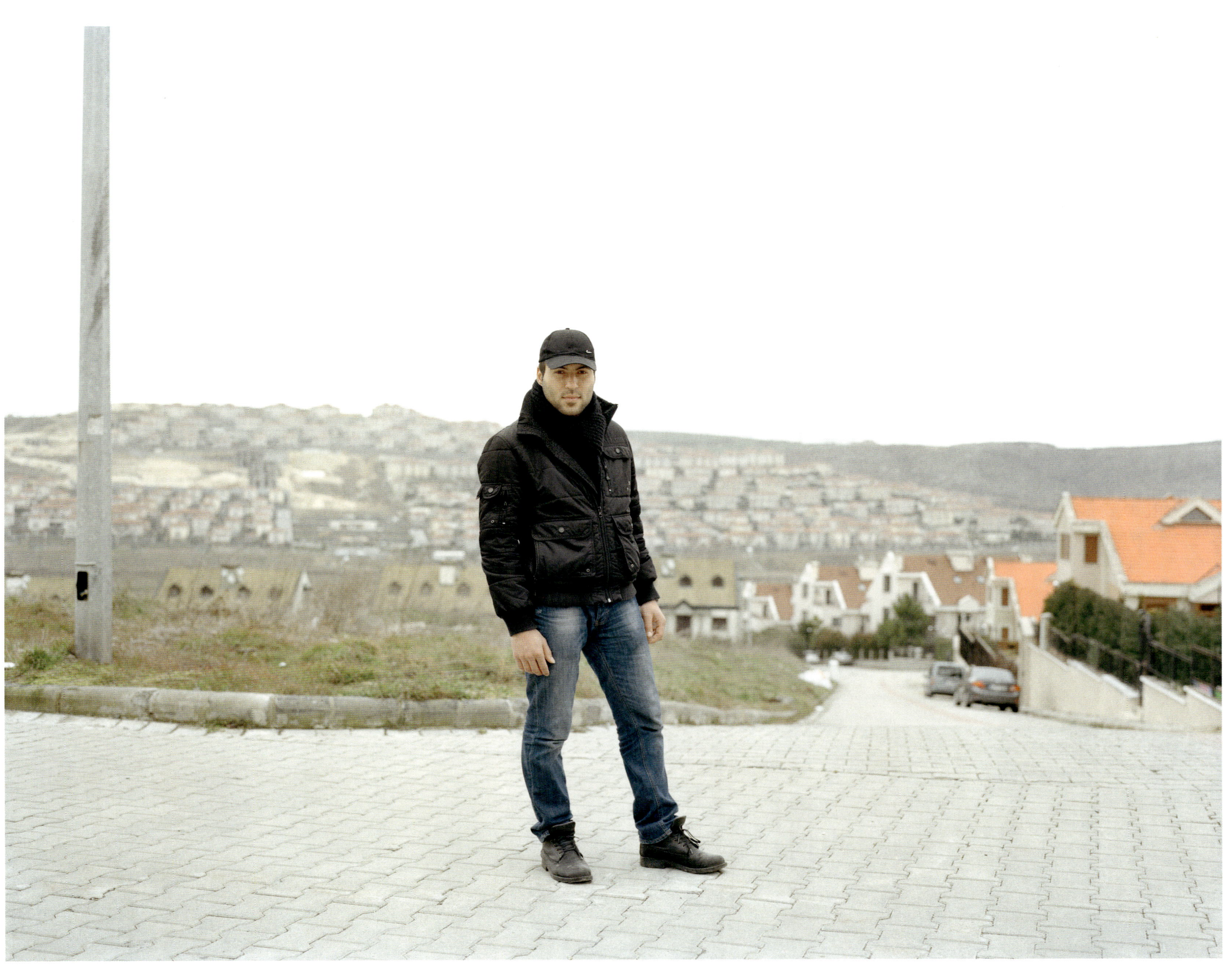

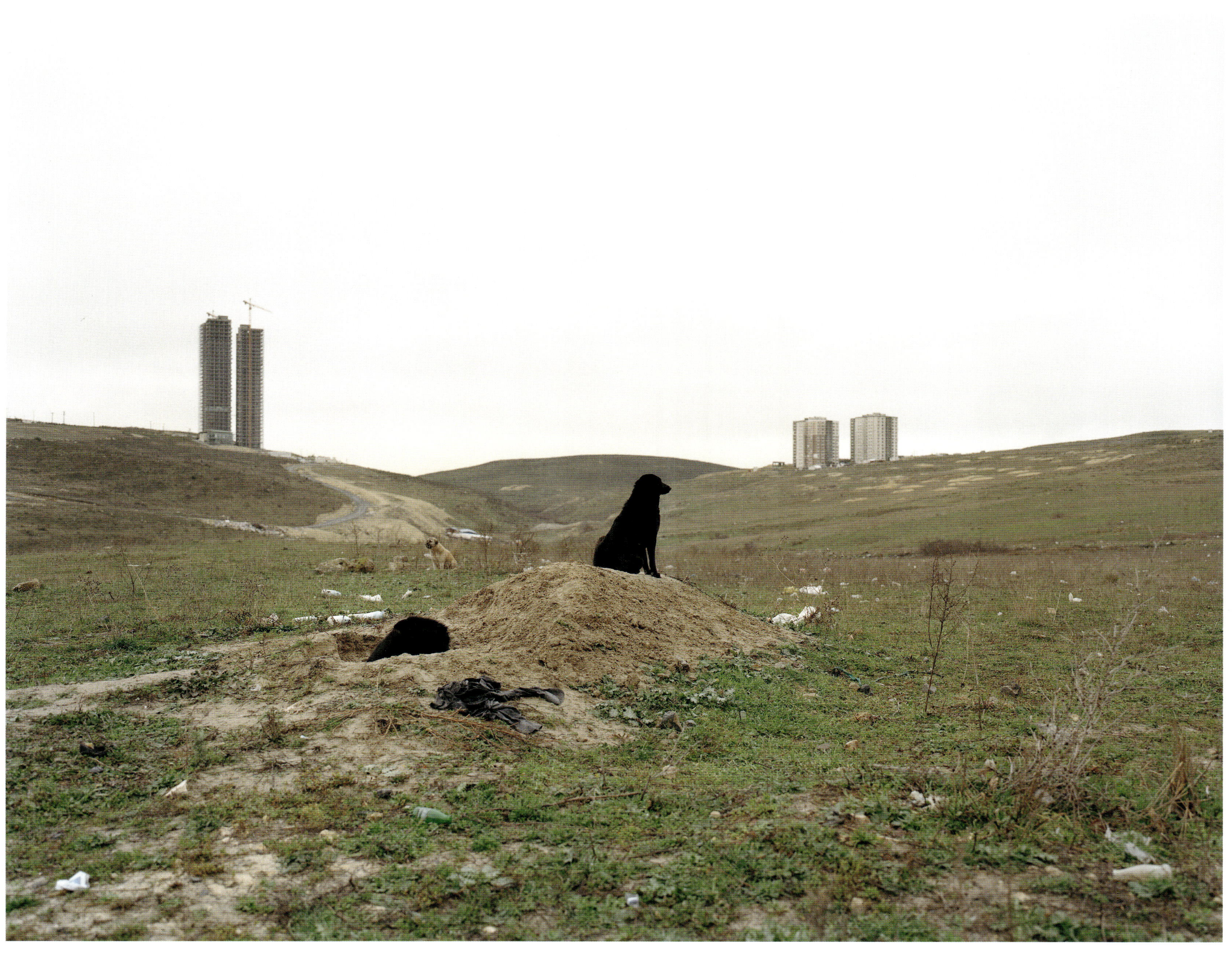

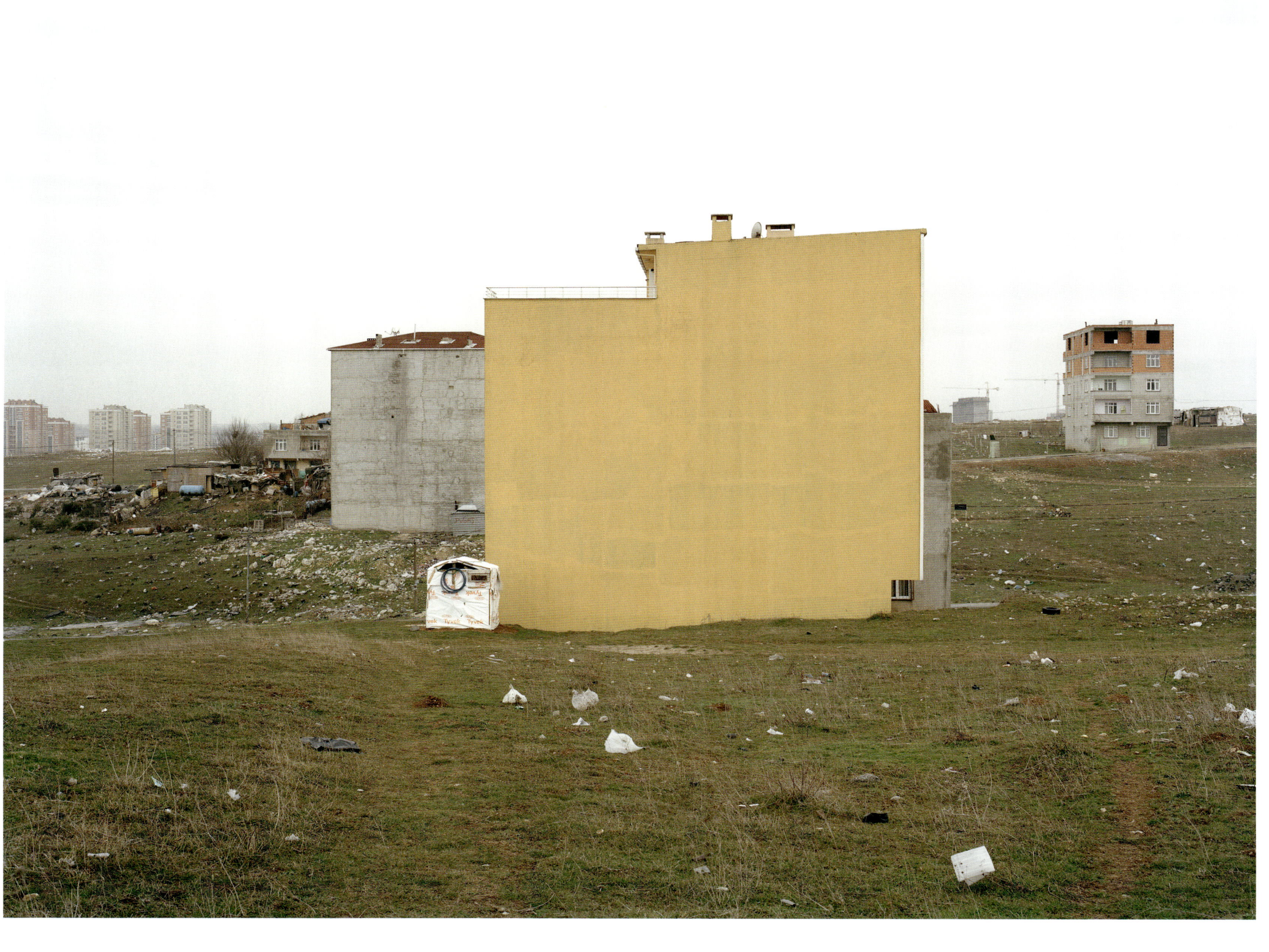

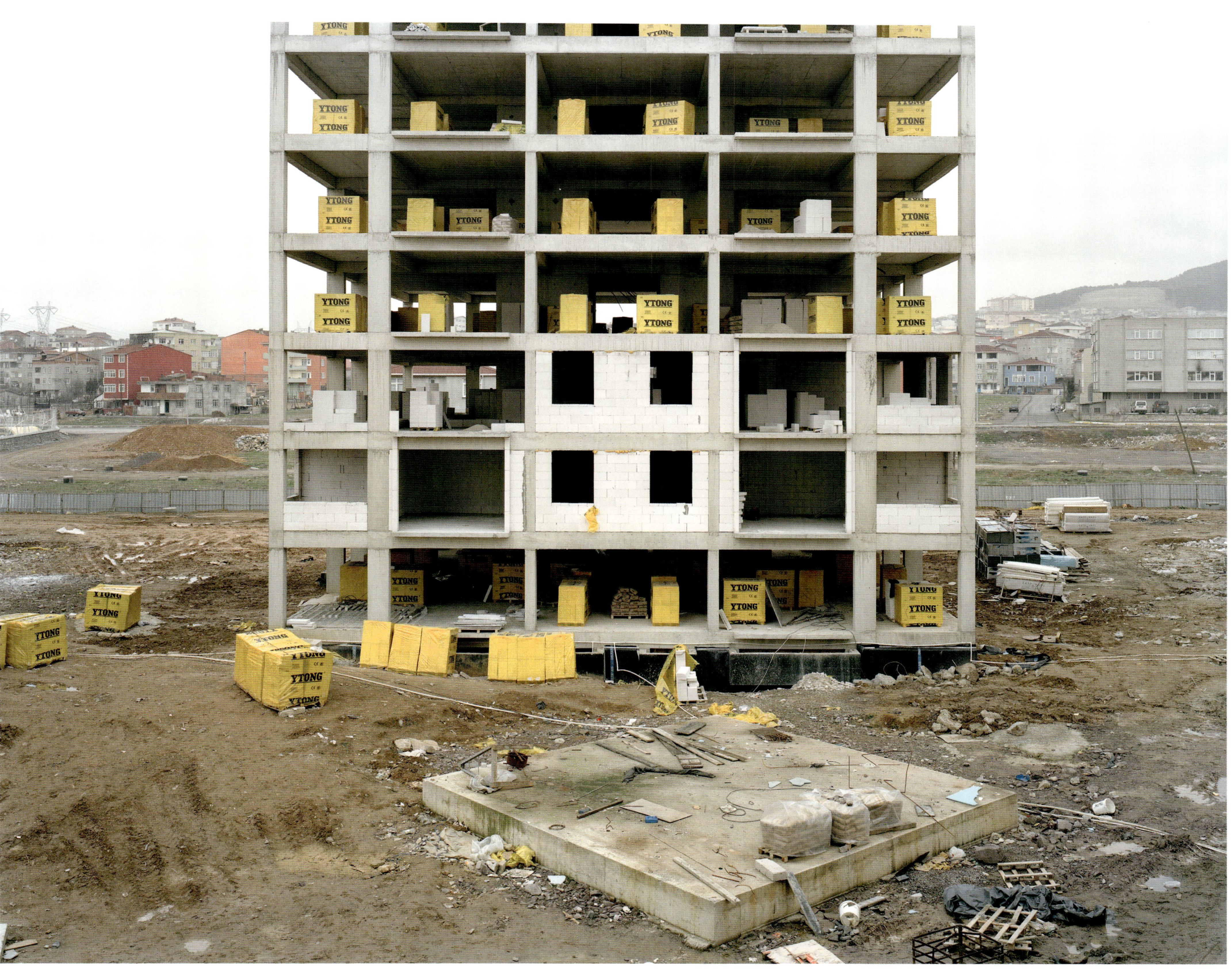

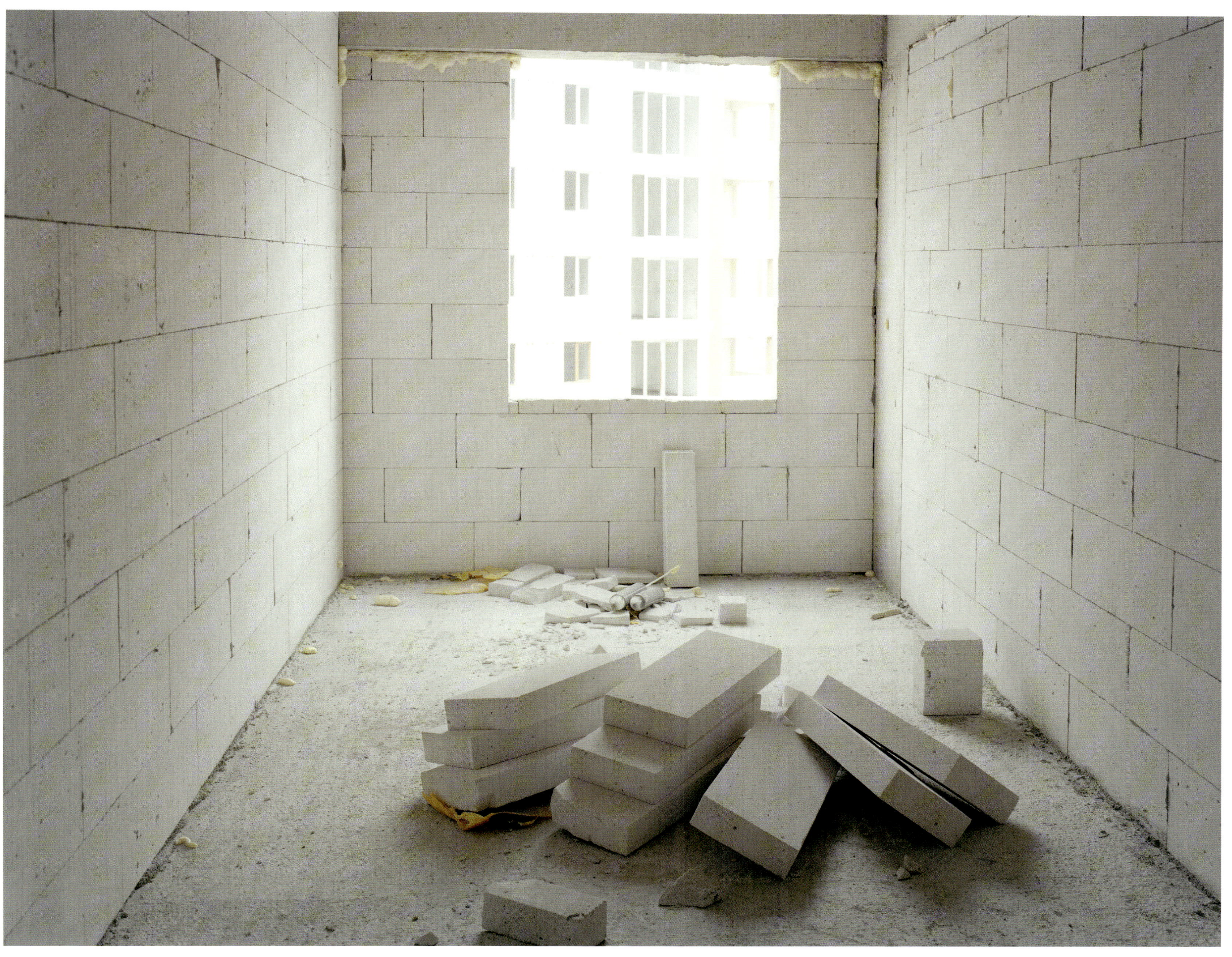

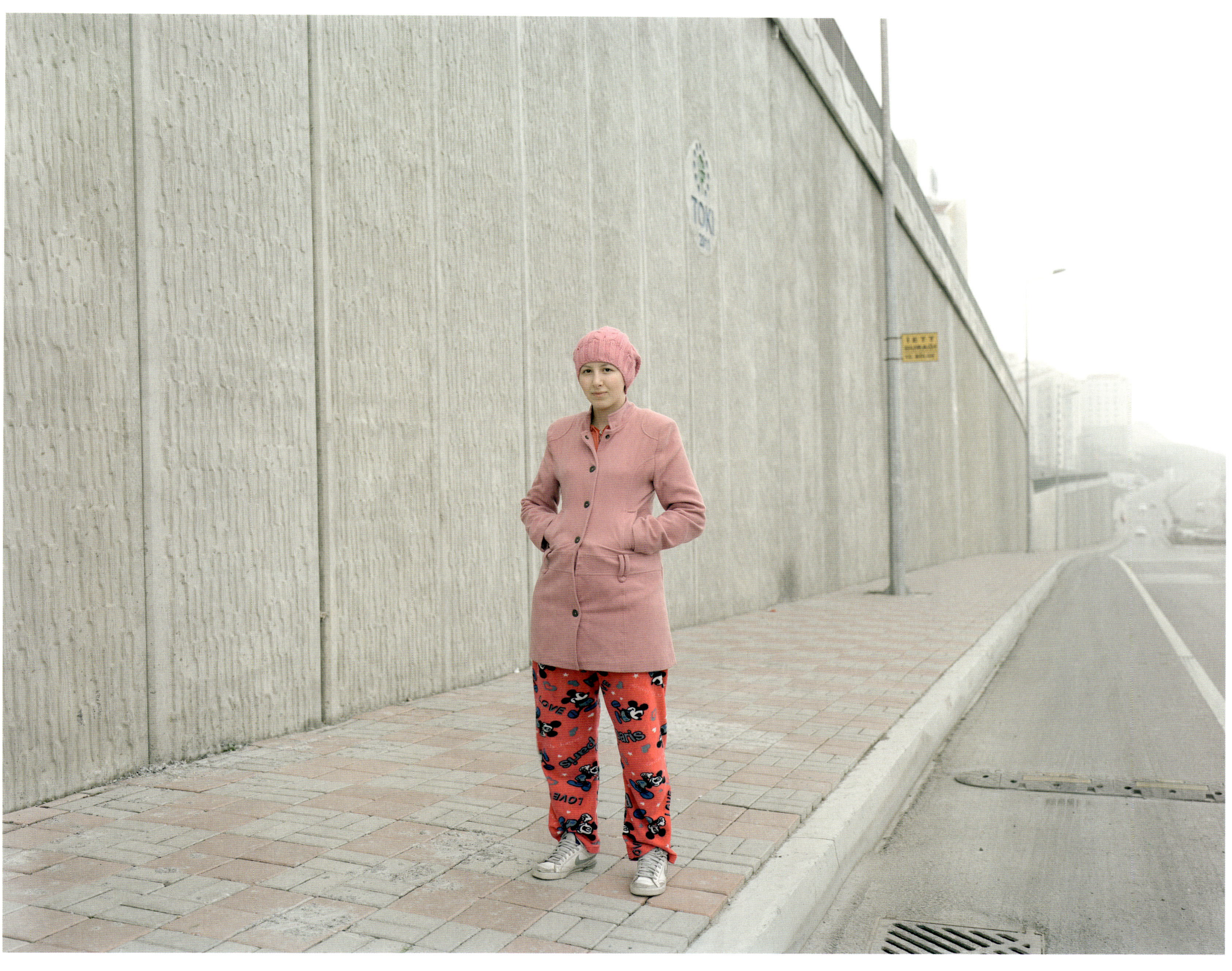
TOKİ

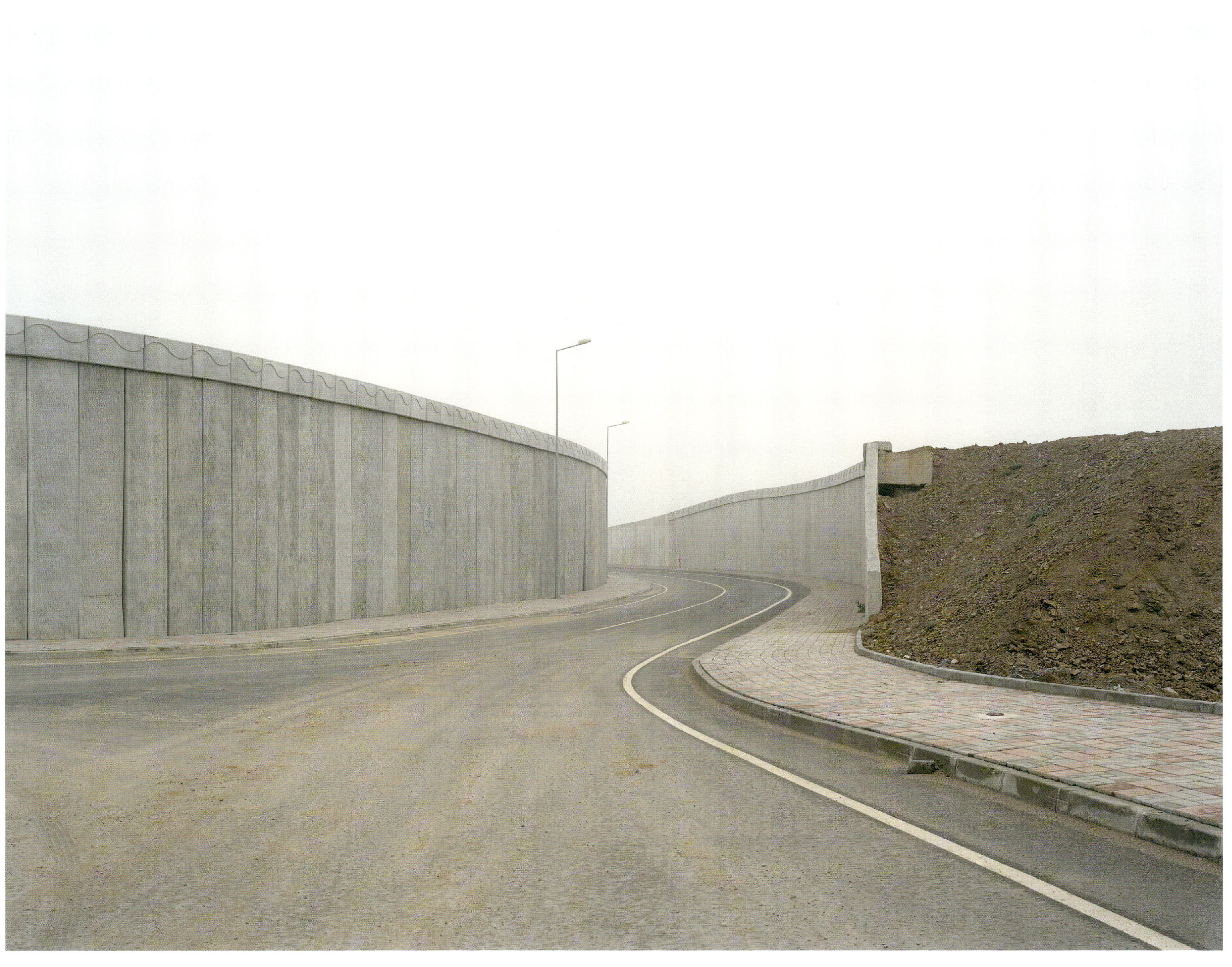

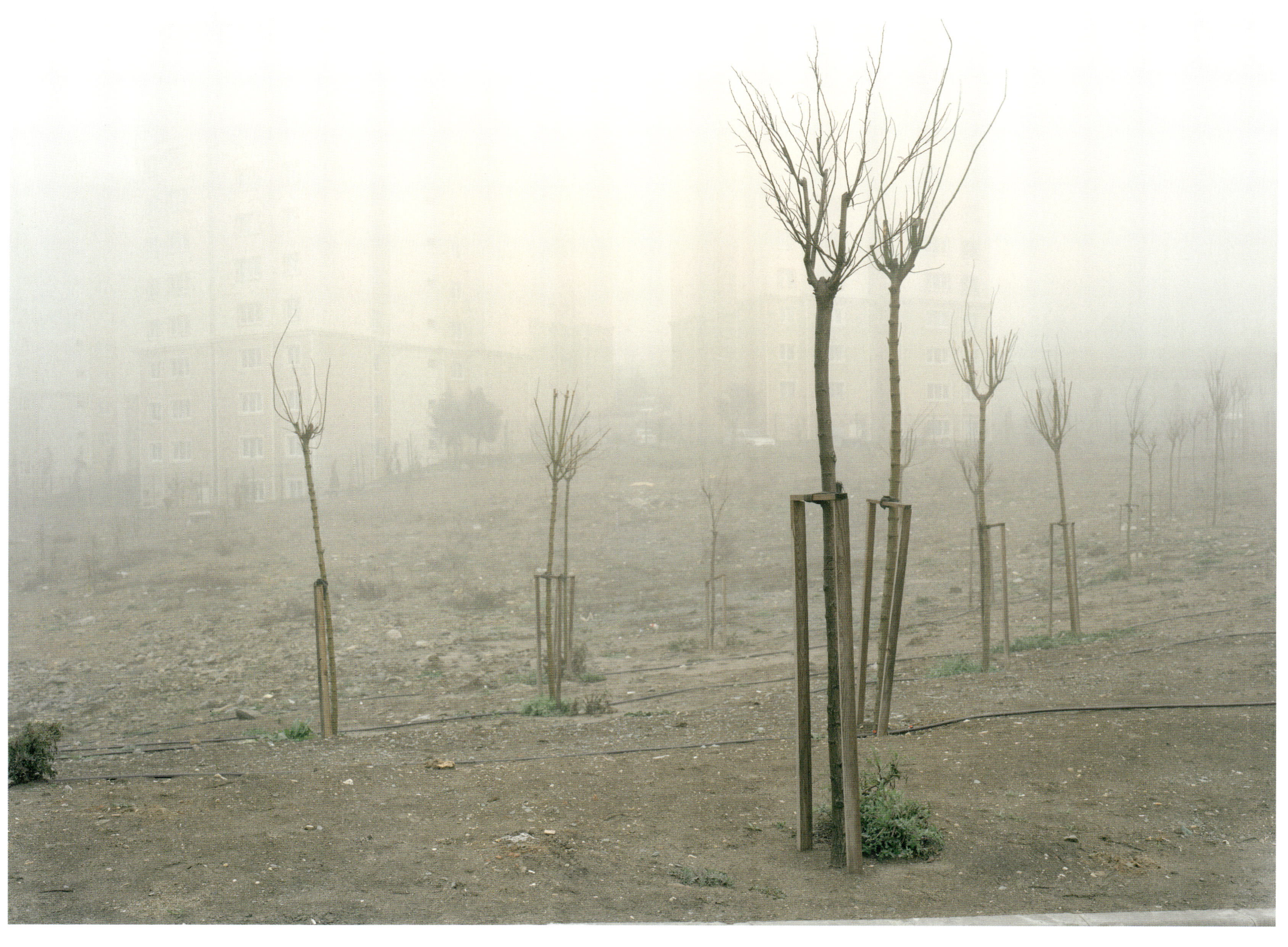

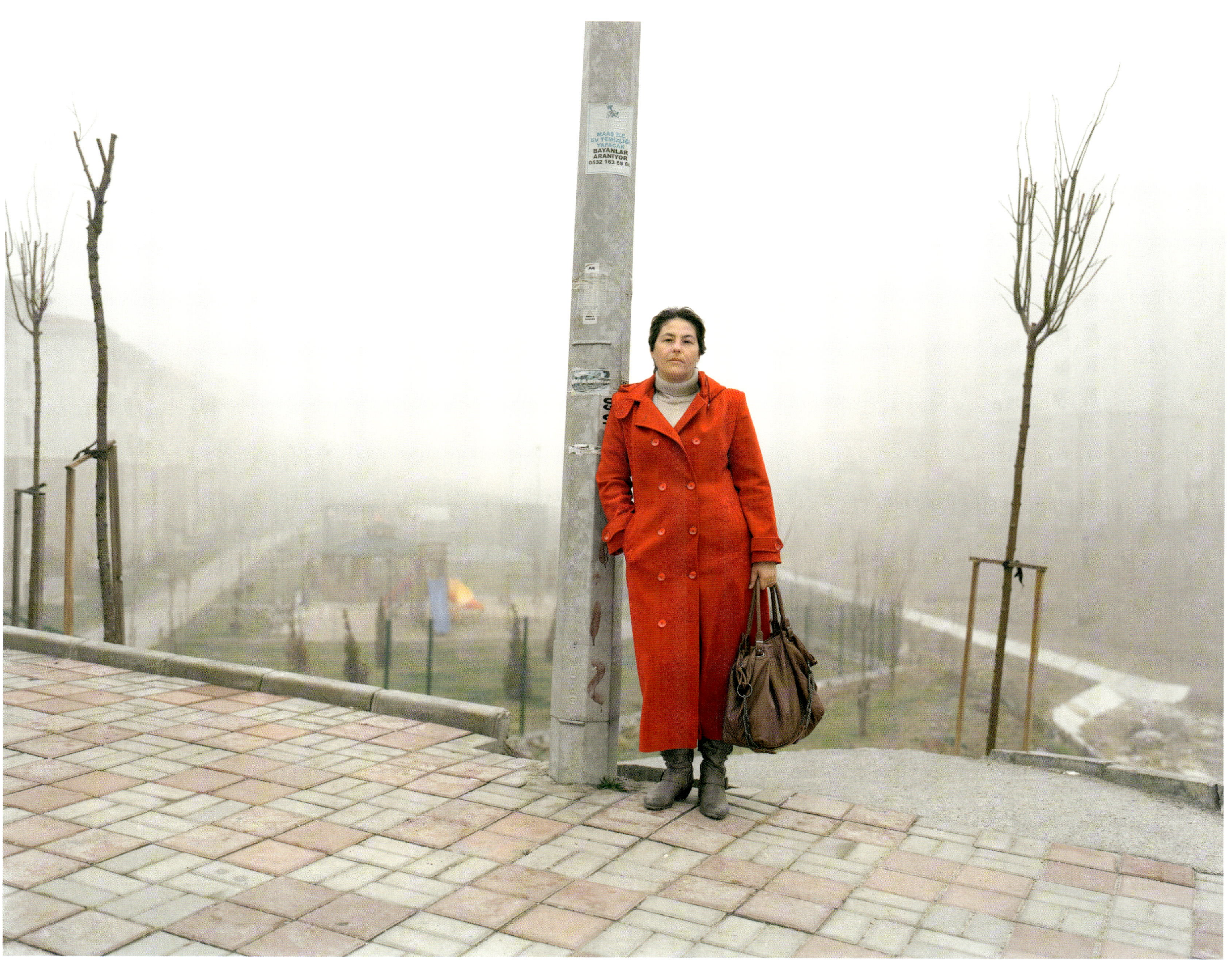

MAAŞ İLE
EV TEMİZLİĞİ
YAPACAK
BAYANLAR
ARANIYOR
0532 163 55 6

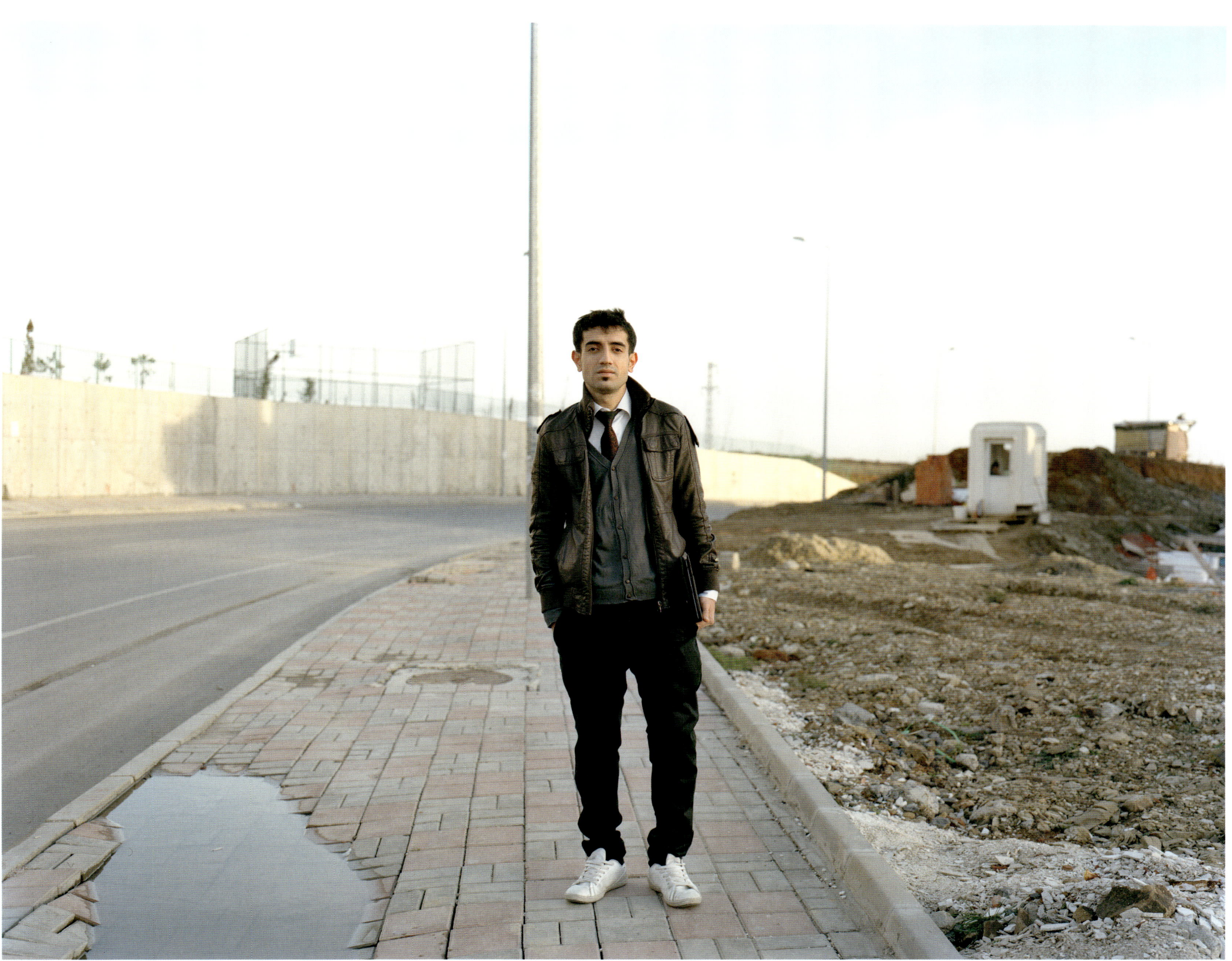

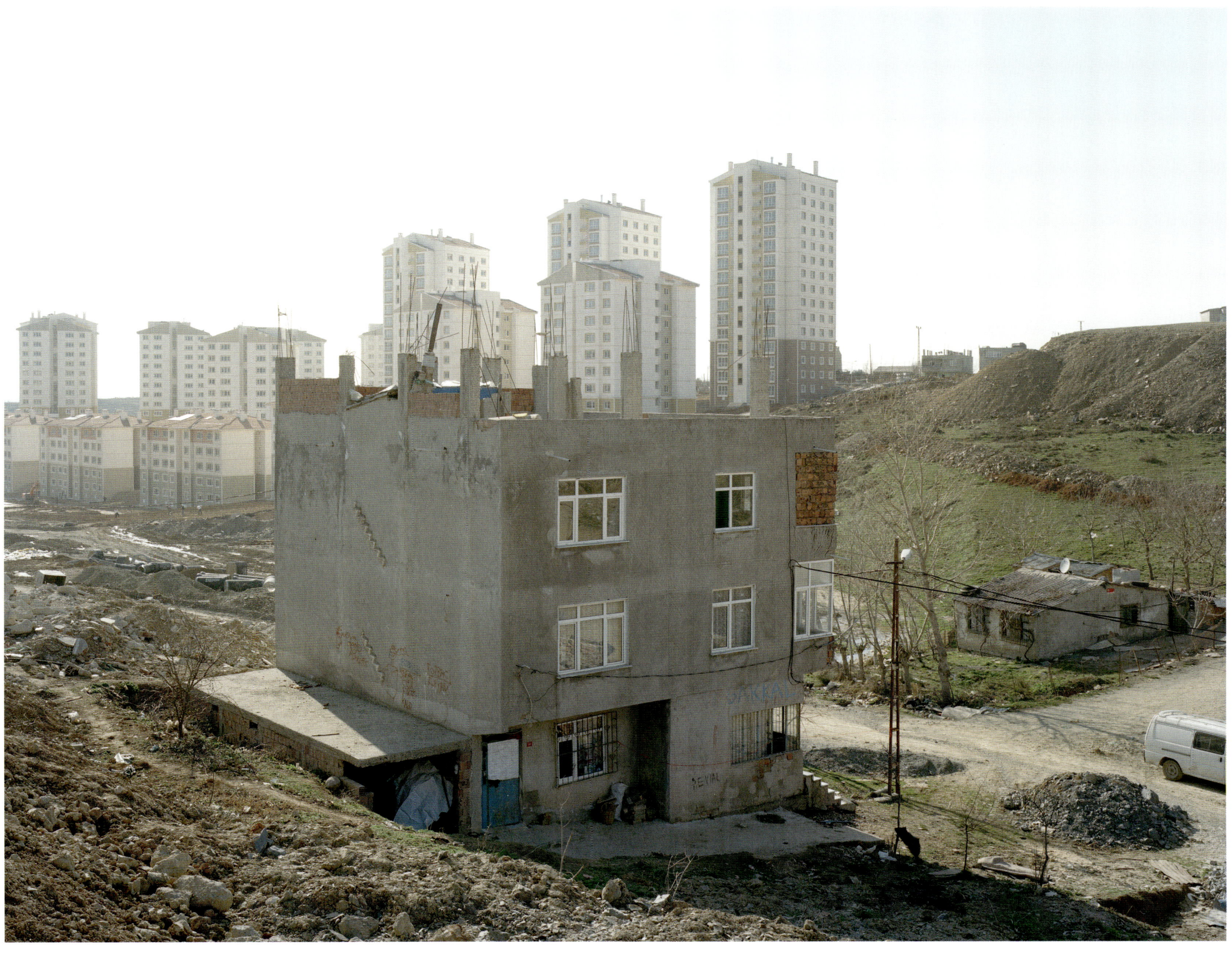

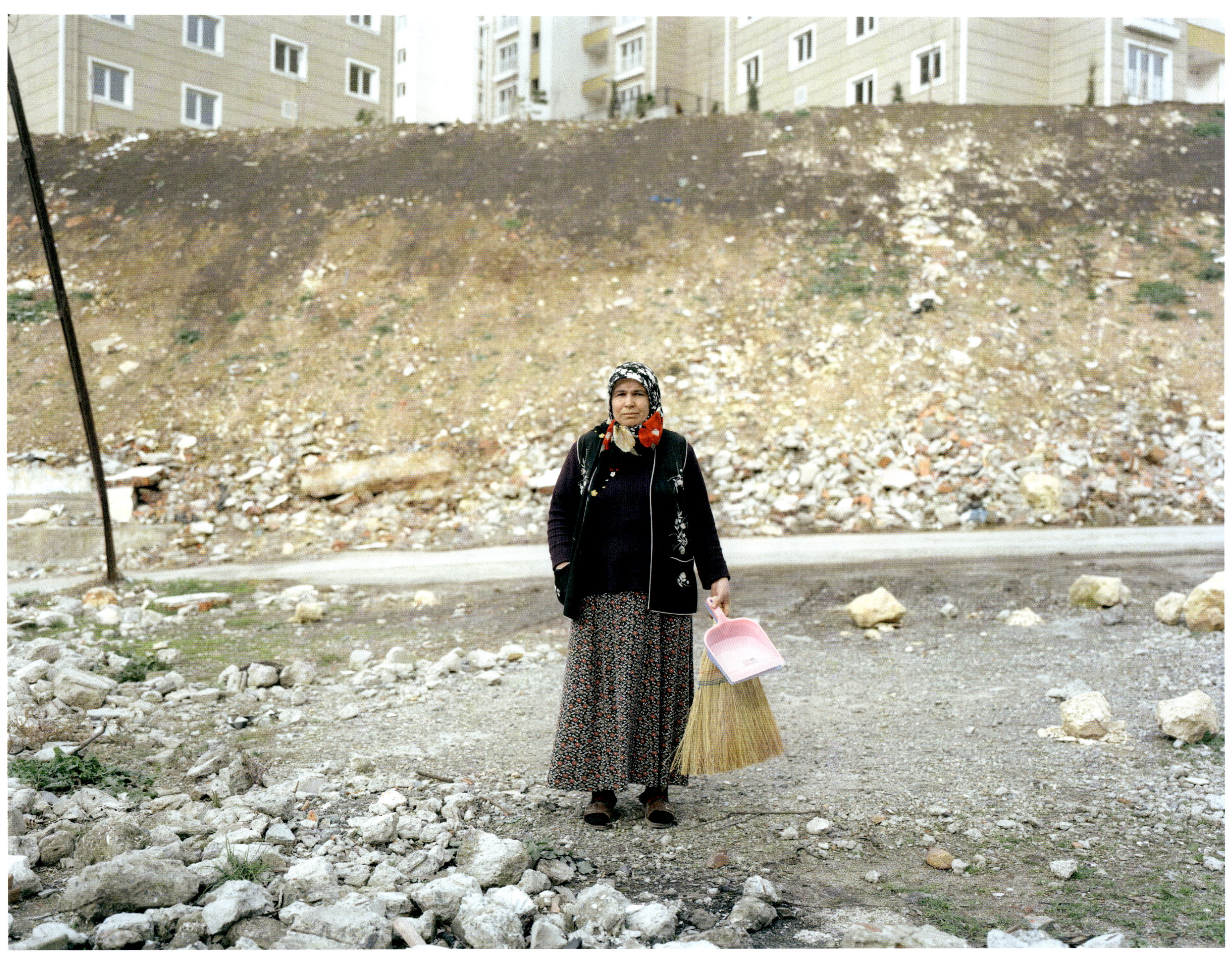

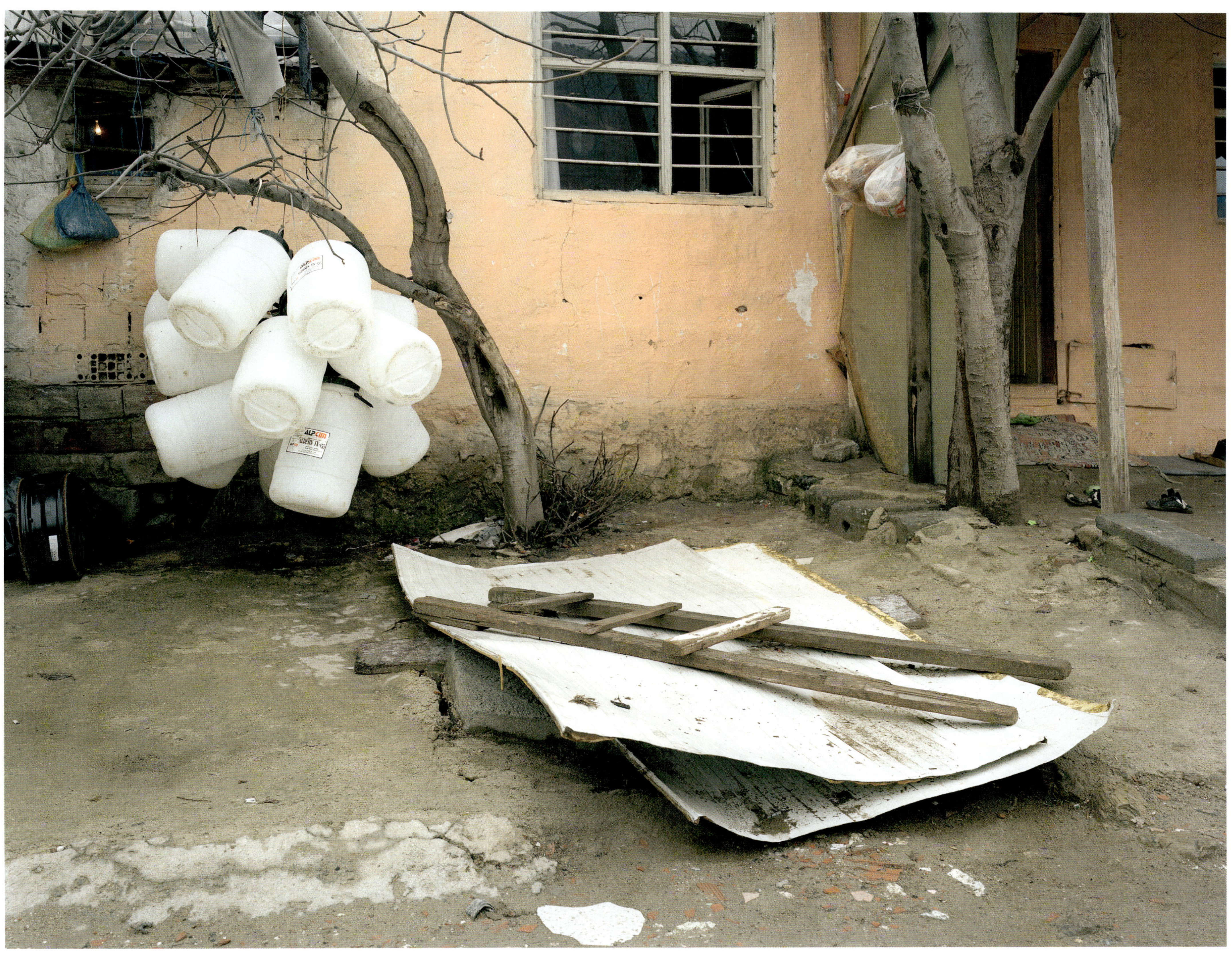

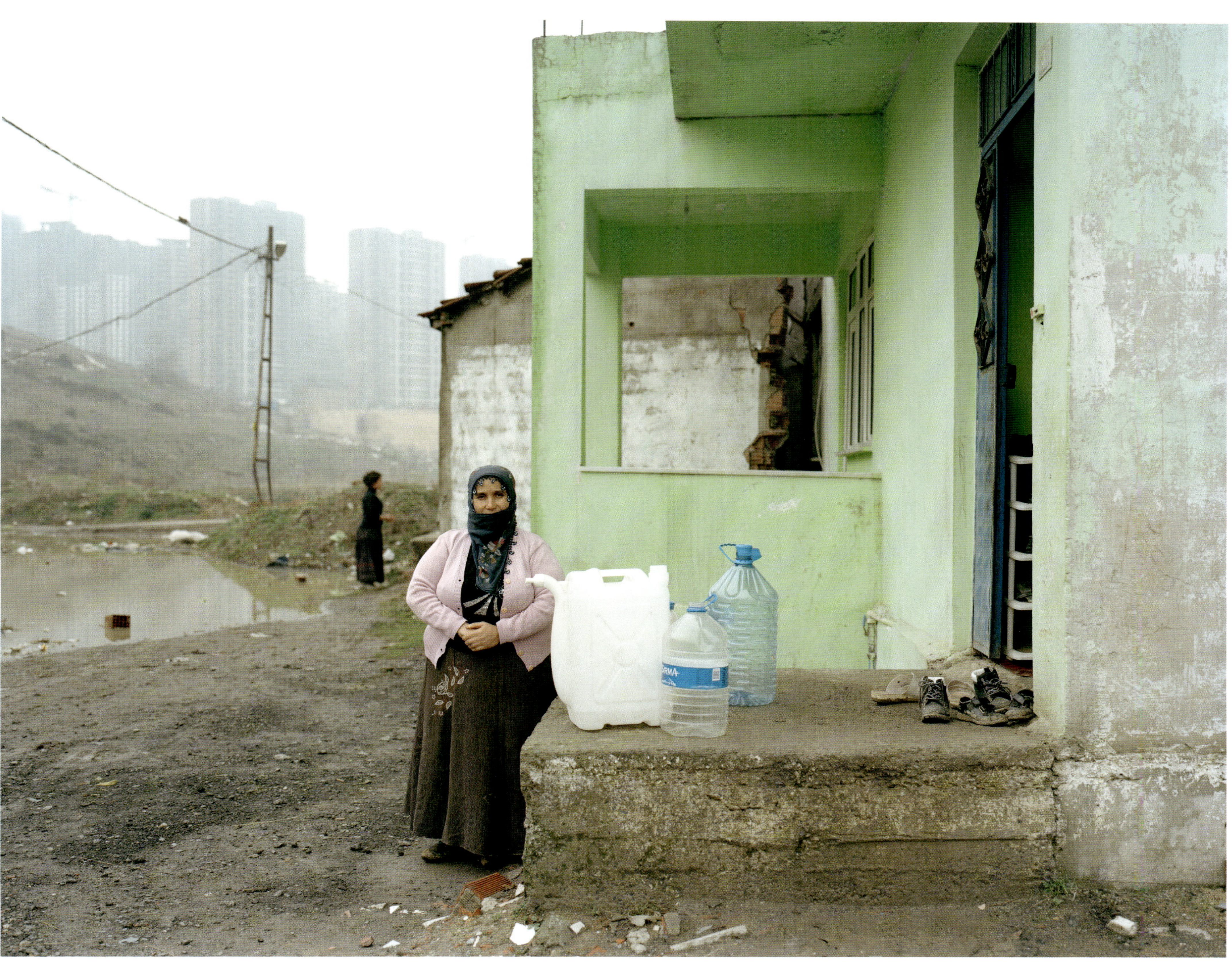

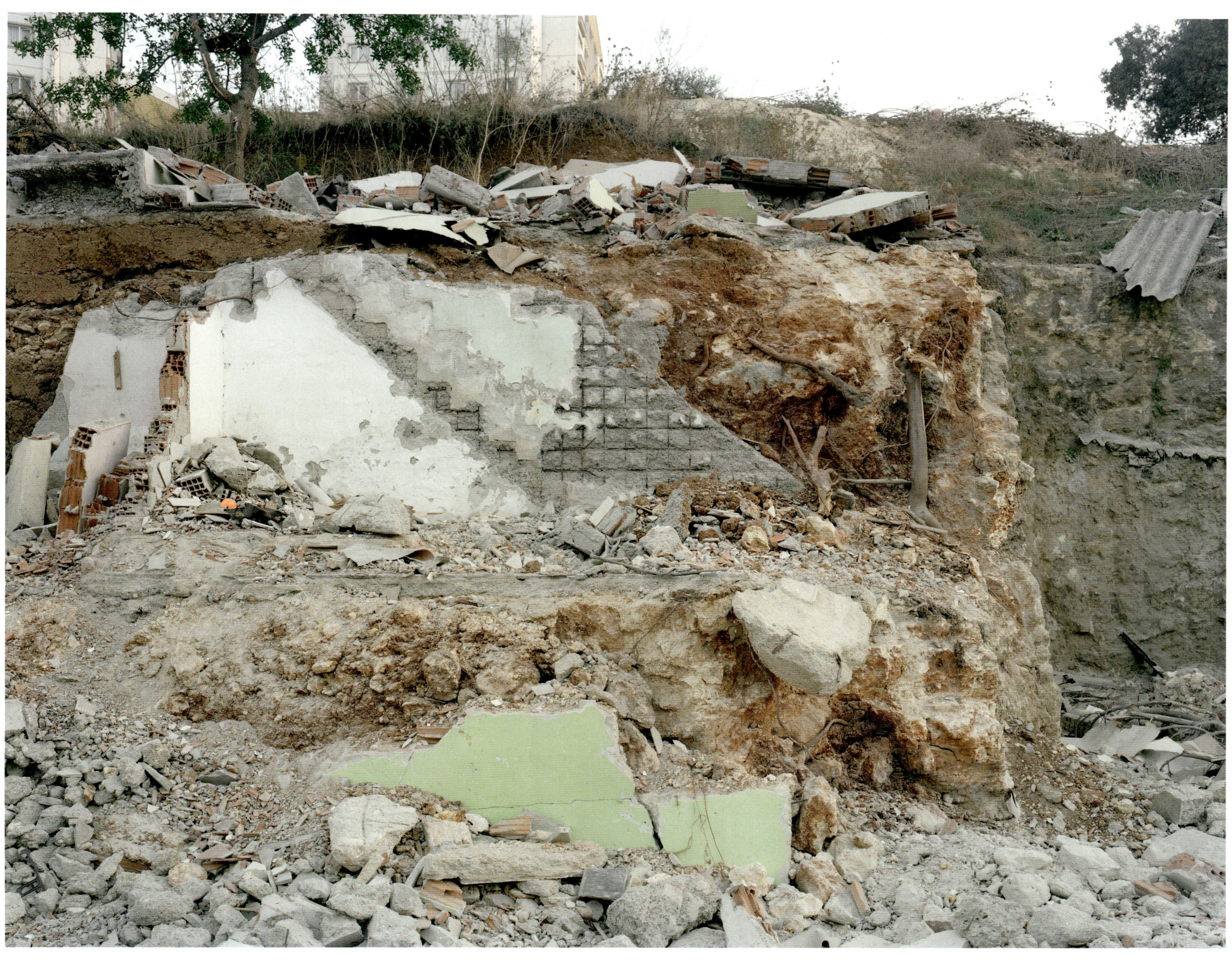

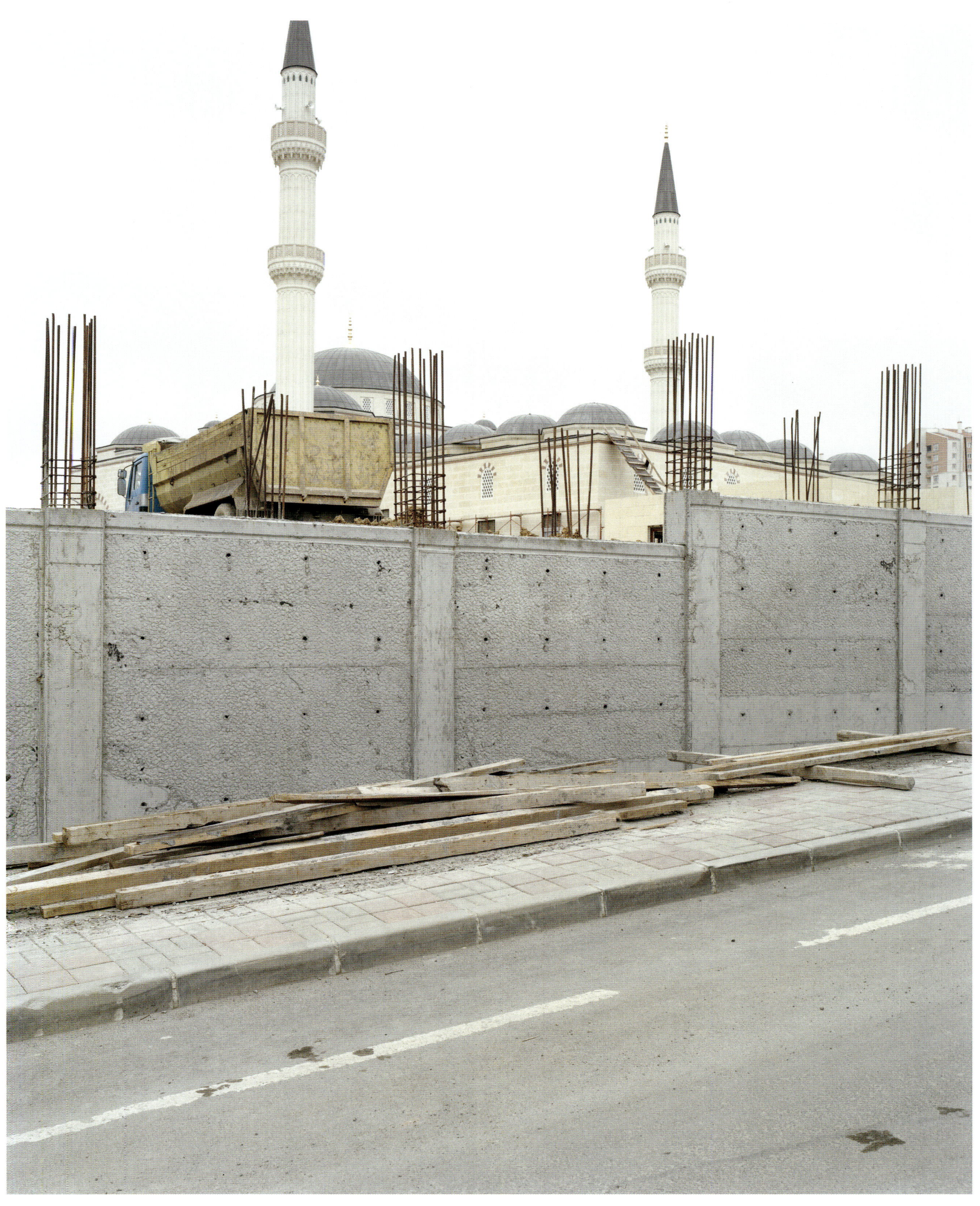

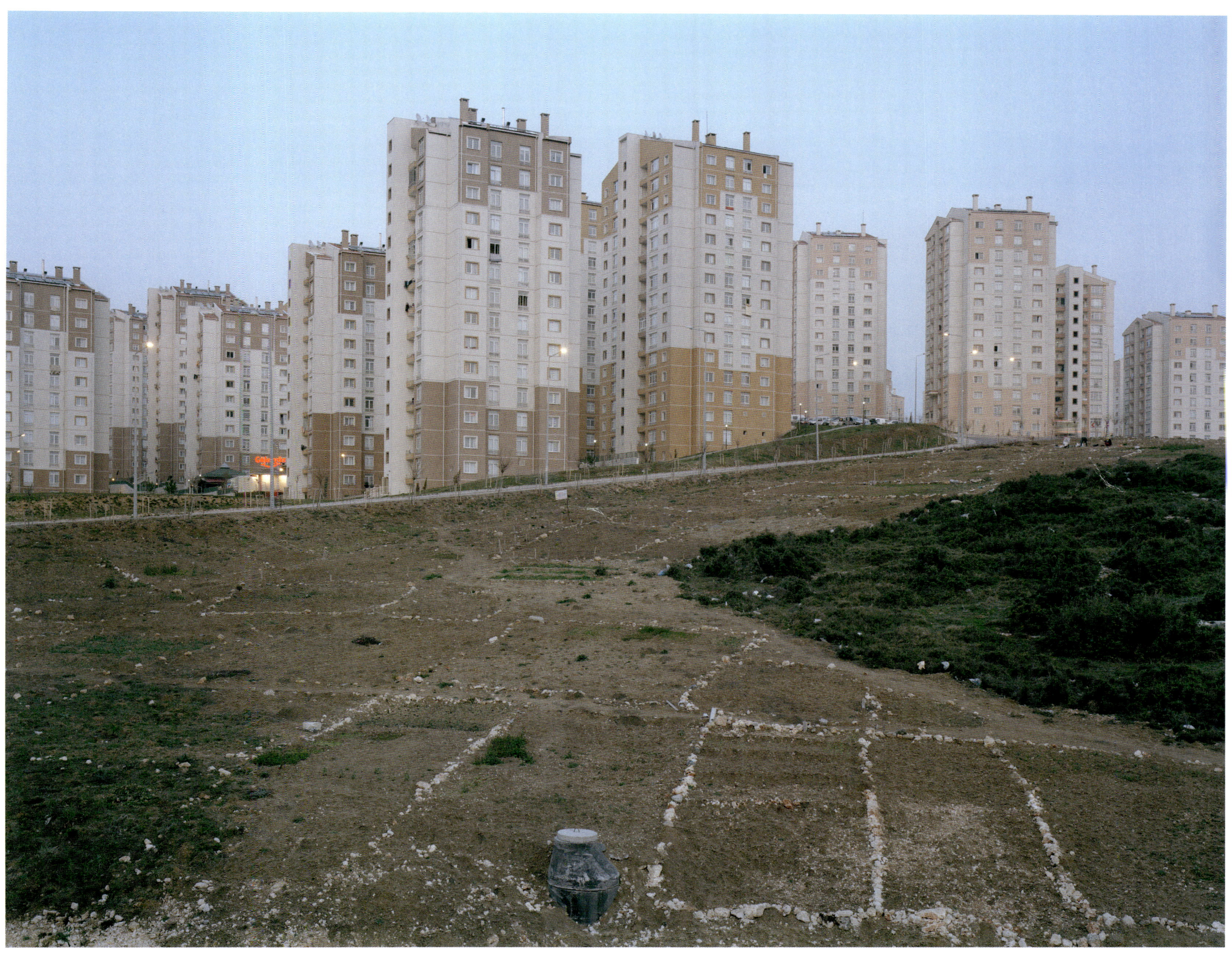

Istanbul now has over 15 million inhabitants, and its geographical position between Europe and Asia makes it a vital point of cultural and commercial contact between the two continents. Its rapid economic and demographic growth has led to great urban transformations, both in areas of the city that were already inhabited and with the adding of entirely new districts.
It is in this context that the radical changes in the scenic and social landscapes manifest themselves, through the birth of new communities and simultaneously the obliteration or metamorphosis of pre-existing ones. Fragile new communities, perhaps still devoid of conflict because of a lack of reciprocal knowledge, form at dizzying speed, and in them the singular of individual lives interacts with the plural of the family (the minimal community) and the randomness of the community.

It is through the medium and guidance of a temporal period that these "new stories" have been created.

The interest is in what happens from the time you begin to plan a new large or medium-sized district or residential area to the time the new community starts from its "zero degree". The photographs are of skeletal houses, men, women, small transitory landscapes, designed and organized enclosed spaces and excluded open spaces, houses, dogs, foundations, walls… There is a powerful, lingering sense of precariousness, instability and bewilderment. The scale on which the pictures are located is that of "trodden" space, where the general themes of the metropolis are brought down from the masses to the individual.

Paola De Pietri (2011)

I have chosen to include in this book Pierpaolo Pasolini's text "Come è mutato linguaggio delle cose" from *Lettere Luterane (1975)*. There is no closed descriptive or comparative intent in this; it is quoted as a source of inspiration to thought and the view of the future.

How the language of things has changed
Pier Paolo Pasolini

from
Lutheran Letters

Before leaving the subject of the "language of things" (which I am sure will have left you vaguely displeased, hostile and perhaps a bit fed up) I want to give you a series of examples which will make you understand a little better what I have been trying to say in this mysterious instructional introduction of mine.

If at your age (and even much later) I walked round the outskirts of a city (Bologna, Rome, Naples), what those outskirts said to me in their coded language was: here the poor live and the life that goes on here is poor. But the poor are workers. And workers are different from you middle-class people. So they want a different future. But the future is slow in coming. So their tomorrow – lived out by them in these outskirts and observed by you – is immensely like today. A today that repeats itself. The sons are assured of an existence similar to that of their fathers. They are destined to repeat and reincarnate their fathers. The revolution is as lazy as the sun that shines on the bare patches of grass, on the huts, on the great peeling buildings. None of this wounds the past, nor does it tear to pieces its values and its models. Urbanism is peasant. The world of the worker is physically peasant; and its recent anthropological tradition commits no transgressions. The landscape can contain this new form of life (shanty-towns, huts, tenement blocks) because its spirit is identical with that of the villages, the peasant huts. The working-class revolution has this same "spirit".

If you walk through the outskirts of a city today those outskirts will say to you in their coded language: "There is no more popular spirit here". The peasants and the workers are "elsewhere" even if materially they still live here. The shanty towns – thank heaven for it – have almost disappeared. But the housing schemes with their great blocks have increased enormously. One cannot speak of an amalgam between them and the old peasant world. Refuse is something frightening and extraneous. The little streams and canals are terrifying. The right of the poor to a better existence had a counterpart which has ended by degrading them. The future is imminent and apocalyptic. Sons are snatched away from similarity to their fathers and projected towards a tomorrow which, while preserving the problems and miseries of today, cannot but be qualitatively different. There is no talk of revolution, least of all when there is frenetic talk about it (a frenzy which the workers' sons have learned in a humiliating manner from the sons of the middle classes. The break with the past and the lack of rapport (even if ideal and poetic) with the future are radical.

So I was brought up by the physical reality of the outskirts of cities to certainty, to a profound, secure and irreplaceable love. You, on the other hand, have been brought up to uncertainty, to a lack of love created by a false,

cruel and pitiless certainty (the "crystallized", conventionalized and blindly
aggressive consciousness of your own rights). I have dwelt on the "language
of the physical reality of the outskirts of cities", but I could have talked
in similar terms of the centres of the cities and of the countryside.

City centres have all his life assured your teacher of the unalterability of the
humanistic tradition and therefore of a quality of life, whether bourgeois
or working-class, which is fundamentally conservative (which the workers'
revolution was to regenerate but not to change). But to you the historical
centres of the cities speak of a particular problem which concerns their physical
conservation, their material survival: the incompatibility between their structure
and the quality of life of a consumerist mass of bourgeoisie and workers
gives birth to a chaos for which neither the word "conservation" nor the word
"revolution" has any longer a meaning.

As for the countryside, the difference between what it taught me and what it
is teaching you is still more enormous. For me it was the certainty of a continuity
with the origins of the human world and gave meaning to each minimal gesture,
to each word, so that they almost acquired the character of a rite. Moreover
it represented to my eyes the spectacle of a perfect world. For you, however,
the countryside speaks of a spectral and almost timorous survival. Its function
(mechanized, industrialized) remains alien to you unless you wish to engage
with it professionally. For the rest, it is an exotic place for atrocious weekends
and for the no less atrocious little villas to alternate with the atrocious flats
in the city (all atrocious to me, naturally).

You will understand gradually in the course of these lessons, dear Gennariello,
that in spite of appearances these talks of mine are by no means panegyrics
of the past (which in any case I did not much like when it was the present).
They are different from anything a man of my age can say today: they are
talks in which "conservation" and "revolution" are words which no longer have
meaning (so, you see, I am modern too).

I see, however, that even this page of examples continues to remain vague
and general. Therefore next time I shall speak to you about a concrete example:
I shall talk to you about the city of Bologna.

1 May 1975
Translated from the Italian by Stuart Hood

Come è mutato
il linguaggio delle cose
Pier Paolo Pasolini

da
Lettere luterane

Prima di abbandonare il capitolo sul "linguaggio delle cose" (che son sicuro
ti avrà lasciato vagamente scontento, ostile e magari un po' "scocciato") voglio
darti una serie di esempi che ti faranno capire un po' meglio cosa ho voluto
dire con questo mio esordio pedagogico misterioso.

Se io alla tua età (e anche molto dopo) camminavo per la periferia di una città
(Bologna, Roma, Napoli…), ciò che quella periferia mi diceva "in suo latino" era:
qui abitano i poveri e la vita che vi si svolge è povera. Ma i poveri sono operai.
E gli operai sono diversi da voi borghesi. Essi quindi vogliono un futuro diverso.
Ma il futuro è lento a venire. Perciò il loro domani – vissuto in questa periferia
da loro, e da voi contemplato – assomiglia immensamente all'oggi. È un oggi
che si ripete. I figli hanno assicurata un'esistenza simile a quella dei padri.
Essi sono anzi destinati a ripetere e reincarnare i padri. La rivoluzione ha la
pigrizia del sole che splende sui prati spelacchiati, sulle baracche, sui palazzoni
scrostati. Tutto ciò non ferisce il passato, non lacera i suoi valori e i suoi modelli.
L'urbanesimo è ancora contadino. Il mondo operaio è fisicamente contadino:
e la sua tradizione antropologica recente non è trasgressiva. Il paesaggio può
contenere questa nuova forma di vita (bidonville, casupole, palazzoni) perché
il suo spirito è identico a quello dei villaggi, dei casolari. E, appunto, la rivoluzione
operaia ha questo "spirito".

Se invece tu ora cammini per una periferia, sempre "in suo latino" tale periferia
ti dirà: "Qui non c'è più spirito popolare". Contadini e operai sono "altrove", anche
se materialmente abitano ancora qui. Le bidonville (grazie a Dio, certamente)
son quasi sparite. Sono invece enormemente cresciuti i "centri" di palazzoni.
Di un loro amalgama col mondo antico o contadino non si può parlare più.
Le immondizie sono uno spaventoso corpo estraneo. I fiumiciattoli e i canali sono
terrificanti. Il diritto dei poveri a un'esistenza migliore ha una contropartita che
ha finito col degradarla. Il futuro è imminente e apocalittico. I figli sono strappati
alla somiglianza coi padri e proiettati verso un domani che, pur conservando
i problemi e la miseria dell'oggi, non può che esserne qualitativamente del tutto
diverso. Di rivoluzione non se ne parla nemmeno: e tanto meno quanto più
se ne parla freneticamente (una frenesia che i figli degli operai hanno imparato
in un modo umiliante dai figli dei borghesi). Il distacco dal passato e la mancanza
di rapporto (sia pur ideale e poetico) col futuro sono radicali.

Io, dunque, dalla realtà fisica della periferia ero educato alla certezza,
a un amore profondo, sicuro e insostituibile. Tu invece sei educato all'incertezza,
a una mancanza d'amore fatta di una falsa certezza crudele e impietosa

(la coscienza "cristallizzata", convenzionalizzata, ciecamente aggressiva dei propri
diritti). Mi sono dilungato sul "linguaggio della realtà fisica di una periferia
cittadina"; ma discorsi analoghi ti farebbero i centri delle città e le campagne.

I centri delle città, per tutta la vita, hanno sempre assicurato il tuo pedagogo
di una inalterabilità della tradizione umanistica e quindi di una qualità di vita,
sia borghese sia popolare, fondamentalmente conservatrice (che la eventuale
rivoluzione operaia doveva "rigenerare", ma non cambiare). A te invece i centri
storici delle città parlano di un loro problema particolare riguardante la loro
conservazione fisica, la loro materiale sopravvivenza; dall'incompatibilità fra la
loro struttura e la qualità di vita di una massa borghese e operaia consumistica
nasce un caos per cui sia la parola "conservazione" sia la parola "rivoluzione"
non hanno più senso alcuno.

Quanto alla campagna, la differenza fra ciò che essa ha insegnato a me e ciò
che essa sta insegnando a te, è ancora più enorme. Per me essa è stata la certezza
di una continuità con le origini del mondo umano, e ha valorizzato, fino a
dar loro carattere quasi di rito, ogni minimo gesto, ogni parola. Inoltre essa
rappresentava ai miei occhi lo spettacolo di un mondo perfetto. Per te, al
contrario, la campagna parla di sé stessa come di una spettrale e quasi paurosa
sopravvivenza.. La sua funzione (tecnicizzata, industrializzata) ti resta estranea,
a meno che tu non voglia occupartene professionalmente. Quanto al resto, essa
è un luogo esotico per atroci weekend e per non meno atroci villette da alternare
con l'atroce appartamento in città (tutto atroce per me, s'intende).

Capirai piano piano, nel corso di queste lezioni, caro Gennariello, che malgrado
l'apparenza questi miei discorsi non sono affatto lodi del tempo passato
(che io, in quanto presente, non ho del resto mai amato). Sono discorsi diversi
da tutto ciò che oggi da parte di un uomo della mia età si possa dire: discorsi in
cui "conservazione" e "rivoluzione" sono appunto parole che non hanno più senso
(come vedi sono, dunque, moderno anch'io).

Mi accorgo tuttavia che anche questa mia pagina di "esempi" continua
a mantenersi nel vago e nel generico. Perciò la prossima volta ti parlerò
di un esempio concreto. Ti parlerò, cioè, della città di Bologna.

1° maggio 1975

Istanbul
New Stories.
On Paola De Pietri's
Photographs

Necmi Sönmez

"In conclusion: in order to teach man, to see
from new angles, ordinary subjects should
be photographed from unusual positions and
new subjects from different angles, whereby
the photographer tries to create a complete
picture of the subject."[1]

Alexander Rodchenko

A city in constant flux, Istanbul began to grow in an unprecedented manner in the 2000s. The rise of skyscrapers right beside the minarets of mosques that for centuries had defined the texture of the city, was one of the most significant indicators in Turkey in the new millennium. This new development did not only completely erase traces of the "picturesque Istanbul"[2] produced from the 18th century on by the dreams and fantasies of Western writers, but it also revealed the radical nature of the change the city was undergoing. Thus, the appearance of the city changed entirely, and first and foremost the silhouette of the old harbour area, and the landscape of the Bosphorus coast and the Golden Horn. Areas in the periphery of the city, used only as agricultural land in the past, were opened to settlement, satellite cities formed entirely of high-rise buildings sprung up on land in both the European and Asian parts of the city. These areas, developed with no clear "urban planning" and lacking necessary infrastructural services, were at least two to three hours away from the city centre. Walled communities that increased the capital accumulation of the circle around political power thanks to the system of exploitation introduced by neo-liberalism, and skyscrapers rising in the centre of Istanbul without planning permission became the symbol of the destruction of "urban texture" through the pillaging of public land. The first decade of the 21st century in Turkey reads like a short history of the structural malfunction during which the social and economic rights of workers, pensioners and low-income earners were removed by what has been described as "neo-liberalism with a religious hallmark"[3].

One of the most significant drivers of neoliberal restructuring is TOKI, a state institution that develops satellite cities[4]. With TOKI building one satellite city after another, housing tens of thousands of people along the periphery of Istanbul, the city began to rapidly grow to become a "megapolis" of twenty million people, including unregistered and unregulated inhabitants. Parallel to this, further estates developed by holdings supported by the government accelerated the waves of "internal migration" to Istanbul. A veritable heaven on earth was being offered in these new walled communities with swimming pools, Turkish baths and sports facilities with separate sections for men and women to the *nouveau riche*, conservative masses, the majority of which had come from the Anatolian heartland. As one of countless foreign words introduced into Turkish, the term "rezidans/residence"[5] used to market this type of housing unconditionally expressed social inequality. "Satellite cities", rapidly rising along the periphery of Istanbul as a model for the fast and effective capital transformation, became an icon of the most radical social, economic and political process of change society in Turkey had experienced. This rapid process of shedding skin has been described by many social scientists with the term "New Turkey"[6].

This detailed introduction about the new satellite cities of Istanbul should
not be deemed out of place as I embark on an exploration of the photographs
in Paola De Pietri's series titled "Istanbul New Stories". In this series, De Pietri
adds a new dimension to her "man-made-landscape-change" theme, developed
in her previous series ("Here Again", "La nuova casa", "Vajont" and "To Face").
It is no coincidence that the artist has chosen Istanbul as her theme for her
new series. She gave me an intriguing response when I asked her why she chose
Istanbul for this project:

"The city now has over 15 million inhabitants, and its geographical position
between Europe and Asia makes it a vital point of cultural and commercial
contact between the two continents. Its rapid economic and demographic growth
has led to great urban transformations, both in areas of the city that were already
inhabited and with the adding of entirely new districts. It is in this context that
the radical changes in the scenic and social landscapes manifest themselves,
through the birth of new communities and simultaneously the obliteration
or metamorphosis of pre-existing ones. Fragile new communities, perhaps still
devoid of conflict because of a lack of reciprocal knowledge, form at dizzying
speed, and in them the singular of individual lives interacts with the plural
of the family (the minimal community) and the randomness of the community."[7]

The "Istanbul New Stories" series comprises forty-four compositions shot
in 2012-2013, focusing first and foremost on the impact of landscape transformed
by human intervention. Since De Pietri treats her subject matter not from
a documentary but a "conceptual" point of view, we observe an approach devoid
of sentimentality, or an effort to document. Departing from different points,
the artist's compositions bring together the "life in the new communities"
in a non-indexical and non-chronological manner. Here, viewers observe
the various stages of the construction of buildings, the interior and exterior
of apartment blocks, but also, ultimately, the main context that surrounds these
photographs: new life-style models. This approach, which consciously avoids
narrative, praise or criticism, is the outcome of De Pietri's conceptual standpoint.
By focusing in her photographs on the impact on individuals of life in the satellite
cities of Istanbul, the artist reveals certain "boundary points". The interior,
exterior, gardens, walls and roads of satellite cities are frequently emphasized
elements in the compositions. Figures located around these boundary points
bear the anxiety of being "new" in a place. In her works, De Pietri invites viewers
to the "conditio humana" of individuals confronting new models of life.

One must not forget that until the 1960s, more than half of Turkey's population
lived in rural areas.[8] By the 2000s, the balance had changed. The majority
of the population now lived in cities.[9] The satellite cities and walled communities
of Istanbul, Turkey's centre of attention, became the symbol of the "new model
of life". In her photographs, De Pietri is interested in how these buildings
are not mere constructions, but have assumed different metaphorical values.
Satellite cities, featuring all sorts of comforts from tennis courts to swimming
pools, billiard halls to artificial lakes did not only offer a luxurious life
style to their inhabitants. It wasn't easy for individuals, who as recently as a
generation ago were engaged in deeply-rooted relationships in villages, towns
or neighbourhoods, where a different type of social life takes place, to get used
to the "new model of life" in these estates. The viewpoint De Pietri develops
allows her to focus on interrupted "human relations" without getting caught up
in details. "Neighbourhood relations" which have an almost sacred significance
for families in Turkey have been entirely abolished in the model of life in place in

skyscrapers. Proverbs in Turkish such as "Don't buy a house, make neighbours," denoting the first importance given to neighbours and "One neighbour is in need of the ashes of another," denoting that even in the smallest matters one neighbour can help another emphasize the importance of the social aspect of life. However, modern life in the residences which is based on "ignoring one's neighbour" lifted the last archaic layer off society in Turkey. The "new stories" in De Pietri's compositions contextualize the interrupted social life of individuals in detail.

A quarter of the "Istanbul New Stories" series shows individuals standing in front of various backgrounds. A careful examination of these compositions reveals that these full body figures of different ages and gender framed by architectural components display almost a statuesque posture. The "solitude" perceived in these images displaying an ordinary moment in everyday life is loaded with metaphors. These "moments of solitude", interpreted by De Pietri with special interest excluding emotional, theatrical and romantic qualities, have a distinct meaning for society in Turkey. Entering the 20th century without significant industrialization, the strong social ties of society meant that "individualization" was postponed. However, the new model of life on the estates has by-passed mechanisms of social control (such as family, environment and group of friends) and enforced the "obligation to be alone" upon individuals. De Pietri's full-body figure compositions focus not on the facial expressions of individuals but on their postures, and body shapes. Each dressed in accordance with a different worldview; these figures are a sign that the new model of life in estates also brings together different life styles. This life, perceived as a form of social climbing and progress, enabled a meeting under the same roof of different political, social and ethnic groups, which otherwise would not come together. De Pietri's figures appear before their viewers as sensitive portraits of individuals whose process of becoming social has been interrupted.

The "Istanbul New Stories" series displays sensitivity towards the stray dogs living around these estates as much as it does towards their human inhabitants. Dogs are the main subject matter of two compositions, and appear frequently in other photographs, too. Trying to keep up with the changes in life, they, too, like the inhabitants of the community, do their best to build "their own living space", at times closer to, and at times away from humans. The similarity between stray dogs and humans is striking, because the stories of stray dogs that live in the areas around big cities are as rich as those told by the inhabitantsof these walled communities.

We could think that the stories that lend their name to Paola De Pietri's new series are founded on sentiments of identity and belonging. Considering that every individual has his or her own unique story, we can comprehend how difficult it is to assemble their stories under a common denominator. Yet, is there not a common, specific spine to all these stories that emerge in mega metropolises across the world in different cultural frameworks, whether it is Istanbul, Shanghai, or São Paulo? Every individual who is forced to move and build a new life has to form some kind of new harmony between himself or herself and the new environment in order to attain happiness. Paola De Pietri's photographs provide highly significant fragments of data regarding the conditions and self-sacrificing effort with which this harmony is sought. The real stories, then, are shaped by the ability and intention of those who look at these photographs to perceive and comprehend and isolate.

Düsseldorf, December 2013
Translated from the Turkish by Nâzım Dikbaş

Endnotes

1 Alexander Rodchenko, "The paths of modern photography" (*Novyi Lef*, no. 9, 1928, pp. 31-39) in Selim O. Khan-Magomedov, *Rodchenko The Complete Work*, MIT Press Cambridge, Massachusetts, 1987, p. 225.

2 Istanbul Pittoresque is a concept that emerged as a result of the admiration for Istanbul particularly in Western European countries fuelled by travel books published by European writers and painters who from the 17th century on visited Istanbul. For a more detailed account see: Doğan Kuban, *Istanbul An Urban History*, Economic and Social History Foundation of Turkey, Istanbul, 1996, pp. 336-362.

3 Cihan Tugal, "Occupy Gezi: The Limits of Turkey's Neoliberal Success", http://www.jadaliyya. com/pages/index/12009/occupy-gezi_the-limits-of-turkey%E2%80%99s-neoliberal-succ, accessed on: 15.12.2013; Cihan Tugal, "The Islamic Making of a Capitalist Habitus: The Turkish Sub-Proletariat's Turn to the Market", *Research in the Sociology of Work,* vol. 22, 2011, 85–112, pp. 91-92; Yüksel Akkaya, "Türkiye'de Neoliberalizm, Demokrasi ve Ulus Devlet" [Neoliberalism, Democracy and the Nation-State in Turkey] (10. Ulusal Sosyal Bilimler Kongresi Metinleri [Texts of the 10th National Social Sciences Congress]), Yordam Kitap, Istanbul, 2009.

4 TOKİ, the Housing Development Administration of Turkey, is a state institution founded in 1984. It has been a constant target of criticism since it is directly affiliated with the Prime Minsitry of the Republic of Turkey which holds political power, and because its administration, operational structure and budget audit details are not made public; İhsan Bilgin, "Toki nedir? [What is Toki?]" http://www.taraf.com.tr/ihsan-bilgin/makale-toki-nedir.htm accessed on: 15.12.2013.

5 This term, adapted from the English word "residence" refers to luxurious mansions. However, it has become a topic of humour since even ordinary housing estates are marketed with this word, creating a misleading perception.

6 http://www.euractiv.de/globales-europa/linkdossier/die-neue-tuerkei-000138 , accessed on: 15.12.2013; http://en.wikipedia.org/wiki/The_New_Turkey accessed on: 15.12.2013.

7 Paola De Pietri, "Istanbul New Stories", From the e-mail sent by the artist on 20.3.2013.

8 http://tr.wikipedia.org/wiki/T%C3%BCrkiye_demografisi, accessed on: 15.12.2013.

9 http://tr.wikipedia.org/wiki/T%C3%BCrkiye_demografisi, accessed on: 15.12.2013.

Pier Paolo Pasolini (Bologna 1922, Roma 1975)
was one of the most brilliant and versatile artists
and intellectuals in twentieth-century Italy.
His continual experimentation in the linguistic,
ideological and existential fields led to him being
a poet, novelist, film director, linguist, essayist,
playwright and journalist. He often anticipated
with tragic and lucid foresight the social
and economic changes of the postwar years,
and the advent and rise of the consumer society,
with its limitations, contradictions and idolatries.
Writing poetry and novels was a constant in his
life and led to the publication of some of the most
important works in twentieth-century Italian
literature, such as *La meglio gioventù* (1954),
Le Ceneri di Gramsci (1957), *La religione del mio
tempo* (1961), *Poesia in forma di rosa* (1961-1964),
Trasumanar e organizzar (1971), *Ragazzi di vita* (1955),
Una vita violenta (1959) and *Petrolio*, published
posthumously in 1992.
His rich experience as a director began in 1960 with
Accattone and continued with such films as *Mamma
Roma* (1962), *Il Vangelo secondo Matteo* (1963-
1964), *Uccellacci Uccellini* (1965), *Teorema* (1968),
Il Decameron (1970-1971), *I racconti di Canterbury*
(1971-1972), *Il fiore delle Mille e una notte* (1973-1974)
and *Salò o le 120 giornate di Sodoma* (1975).
The articles he wrote in the years 1973-1975 for the
bourgeois newspaper par excellence, *Il Corriere della
Sera*, were published in two collections: *Scritti corsari*
(1975) and *Lettere luterane*, published posthumously
in 1977. He was murdered on 2 November 1975 at the
Idroscalo of Ostia, near Rome.

Necmi Sönmez (Istanbul, 1968).
Sönmez studied art history in Mainz, Paris, Newcastle
and Frankfurt. He completed his PhD at Johann
Wolfgang Goethe University on Wolfgang Laib.
During the late 80s and 90s, as a successive resident
of many countries, he wrote art criticism
for *Cumhuriyet, Istanbul, Flash Art, Milan* and
Neue Bildende Kunst, Berlin and other publications.
After working as Curatorial Associate at Museum
Wiesbaden, Wiesbaden and Museum Moderner
Kunst Stiftung Ludwig in Vienna, he served
as Curator for Contemporary Art at Museum
Folkwang Essen (2001-2005). After teaching
at Kunstakademie Kassel he became artistic
director at Kunstverein Arnsberg (2005–2008)
and curated exhibitions at the Elgiz Museum of
Contemporary Art, Istanbul and Forum d'Art
Franco-Allemand, Château de Vaudémont. He also
served as a member of the Acquisition Committee
at FRAC Franche-Comté (2008-2010). At present
Sönmez is working as independent curator for
Borusan Contemporary, Istanbul and as programme
consultant at Lepsien Art Foundation in Düsseldorf.

Paola De Pietri (Reggio Emilia, 1960).
De Pietri's projects combine an attentive observation
of landscape and of nature in its temporal dynamics
with the representation of the existential conditions
of human beings. Her work has been exhibited
in solo and group shows at institutions including
the Venice Biennale; Fotomuseum Winterthur;
the Galleria d'Arte Moderna, Bologna; the Museum
of Contemporary Art, Shanghai; the Museo
di Fotografia Contemporanea, Milan; Le Bal, Paris;
the MAXXI, Rome; La Triennale, Milan; the Leopold
Museum, Vienna; the Bozar, Brussels. In 2009
she won the triennial Albert Renger-Patzsch Prize
with the project "To Face".

Acknowledgements

I would like to express my gratitude to the women and men of these portraits for their kindness and cooperation, and to **Özgür Atlagan** for his thorough and professional assistance in taking the photographs.

My particular thanks are due to the institutions and people who have supported the realization of the project and the book with their generous help.

Fotografia Europea
Ağaoğlu Group
Emlak Konut GYO
Lorenza Benvenuto
Fabio Boni
Francesco Caredda
Orhan Cem Çetin
Özgü Özbudak
Cristiana Colli
Galerie Les Filles du Calvaire
Elif Gürbüz
Ute Eskildsen
Franco Farinelli
Marinella Paderni
Galleria Alberto Peola
Cristina Piovani
Marco Rovacchi
Sofia Serin
Necmi Sönmez
Leonardo Sonnoli
Gerhard Steidl
Moira Valeri
Francesca Vezzali
Viviana Vuscovich
Miro Zagnoli
Federica Zanco

"Come è mutato il linguaggio delle cose" (1975) is published by kind permission of Pasolini's heirs and the Garzanti publishing house.

The photographs were taken in 2012–2013.

First edition published in 2017

Book design: Leonardo Sonnoli
Scans by Steidl
Separations by Steidl's digital darkroom

Production and printing: Steidl, Göttingen

Steidl
Düstere Str. 4 / 37073 Göttingen, Germany
Phone +49 551 49 60 60 / Fax +49 551 49 60 649
mail@steidl.de
steidl.de

ISBN 978-3-95829-110-2
Printed in Germany by Steidl